MUSIC
ON
MARTHA'S VINEYARD

Here's to music, Janet
dear friend

Jerry M.

MUSIC
ON
MARTHA'S VINEYARD

A HISTORY OF HARMONY

THOMAS DRESSER & JEROLD MUSKIN

THE
History
PRESS

Published by The History Press
Charleston, SC 29403
www.historypress.net

Front cover, clockwise from top right: Arlo Guthrie, 1979, by Alison Shaw; Alex and James Taylor, 1988, by Peter Simon; The Bodes, 1966 (*clockwise from top left*: Jimmy White, Jack Mayhew, Charlie Leighton and Rick Convery), by Shirley Mayhew. *Courtesy of* Martha's Vineyard Magazine; Vineyard Haven Band, 1899. *Courtesy of Chris Baer.*
Back cover, clockwise from top: United States Slave Spiritual Choir. *Courtesy of Jim Thomas*; Flying Elbows, by Ray Ewing. *Courtesy of the* Vineyard Gazette; "Tivoli Girl." *Courtesy of Martha's Vineyard Museum.*

First published 2014

Manufactured in the United States

ISBN 978.1.62619.623.0

Library of Congress CIP data applied for.

CONTENTS

Contents

PREFACE

Dear Reader:

Tom and Jerry, your authors, took on this writing challenge to understand and then describe things musical as they have evolved on Martha's Vineyard over the decades. We also set out to look at the state of music on the contemporary scene, exploring and describing its antecedents. And acknowledging our predispositions, we explore the special nature of the Island that makes it so compelling to those who create music.

This small island's music was founded in the drumbeats and dances of its first occupants, the Wampanoags, and then from the worship of the devout Christian settlers. Drum and church music are still important elements in the Island's musical life. Early Islanders lived by farming and fishing and then, importantly, by going to sea as crew on whaling ships.

The Vineyard provided many of the whalemen who brought back a tradition of chanteys and sea songs meant to support the difficult work of whaling. Their music was the folk song of the era. To augment the whale ship crews, ships would put into Cape Verde or the Azores to recruit sailors; hence some Vineyard music has a Portuguese influence.

Vineyard whaling captains provided their wives and daughters with pianos. These then served as a basis for music-centered home entertainment and a social life of singing, with additional music offered by various instruments such as guitar, banjo and harmonica.

Church choirs were among the first organized singing groups, and now choral entities, church-related or otherwise, proliferate on the Island. Post Civil War, town bands created community-based entertainment; the prevailing influence of the Vineyard Haven Band is acknowledged. As the Island became a vacation and wedding destination, clubs and bars arose to meet those needs. Prominent among them was the Tivoli dance hall; later musicians performed at such venues as the Chilmark Tavern, the Boston House, the Hot Tin Roof, the Wintertide and the Atlantic Connection. Today, Flatbread, Dreamland, Alex's Place and the Atlantic take center stage, along with the Ritz, the Lampost, the Chilmark Community Center and Featherstone's Musical Mondays.

Many homegrown musicians learned from their parents, teachers and peers. Some left the Island to find fame and fortune but maintained love and respect for the Vineyard. Many more musicians play and sing simply for the love of playing and singing, unconcerned with the larger audience. They find support from a community receptive to folk, jazz, rock, string and choral groups and even ukulele picking.

The Vineyard's musical spectrum has extended itself to include world-class chamber music, popular rock groups and memorable dance bands. Some of the greatest names in music have associations with the Vineyard, including Leonard Bernstein, Beverly Sills and James Taylor.

Vineyard teachers provide buoyant musical support to the young. Some residents offer encouragement in funds and in kind. The local newspapers, the *Vineyard Gazette* and the *Martha's Vineyard Times*, deserve accolades for the supportive nature of their coverage of the music scene. Radio station WMVY, now back on the air, provides announcements and interviews regarding musical events.

It's hard to deny there's something special going on on Martha's Vineyard that makes it a musical mecca. Perhaps it's in the mix of the salt water and the sand or the confluence of weather and ocean currents. Avian flyways alter air currents. Whether it is these factors or something else, there must be something special that makes Martha's Vineyard a magical, musical island.

Throughout our interviews, musicians have rhapsodized about the Island. From that array of encomiums, we can confirm that the Vineyard will be a magnet for joyous music makers far into the future, just as it has been in the past.

This is the poem that launched our effort:

Magical Musical Island

The day joins the calendar like a fine gauze obscuring the surrounding up-island woods, while rendering the seascape beyond into a murky blur.

Day meanders on, opaqueness gives way to translucence then to brilliant clarity.

Stone walls, tree canopied roadways, the roadside offerings of flowers and lowing cattle in the meadow all appear as dazzling epiphanies.

Thoroughbreds on the hill, bicyclists panting up hills and speeding down. Kids rushing to finish their castles before the tide sweeps them away. Kites riding on-shore breezes…

These images, in their totality, in their singularity, magically transform one from the commonplace to the rapture of the here and now…

And the waves pound onto the shore just as a timpani alerts the audience to the opening of a Beethoven opus. "The new day is here!" the pounding surf announces.

Are we to be embraced by a flute day or by a bassoon day? Will the day move on as a spiritual French horn passage or as the mournful drone of a cello?

At evening, will we hear Carly's voice or James's songs? Or Sousa creations at the Rockwellian band concert at Ocean Park? Circuit Avenue is sure to be alive to the pulsing beat of rock and roll.

On certain reverential nights Ravel, Mozart, or Brahms will be cascading from the open windows of the Old Whaling Church.

The Vineyard fairly bursts with the sounds of music. The Island's visual feasts are in harmony with the grandeur and pervasiveness of its music. It is as if one united with the other in a pact with angels.

The blessed culminations of this synergy is our magical, musical island.
—written by Jerry Muskin for the dedication of the fortieth anniversary of the Martha's Vineyard Chamber Music Society in 2010. This poem was published in Meanderings, *a poetry book by Jerry Muskin.*

"The hills are alive with the sound of music." Nowhere is this statement truer than on the island of Martha's Vineyard, a small speck of land off Cape Cod. Sante Fe, Newport, Wolf Trap, Rockport and Tanglewood are centers of music, but they are time limited and site specific. When summer is over, most players from these musical enclaves return to their gigs, orchestral chairs or recording studios. New Orleans qualifies as a year-round locus of great music performed by unsurpassed musicians of their musical genre—Dixieland jazz—but it is essentially a singular style. On the Vineyard, the summer season of music lasts all year long, all over the Island, in churches, private homes, coffeehouses, clubs and prime music venues.

Great musicians are on-Island in all seasons. Many are full-time residents with full-time jobs but part-time musical opportunities. Some are professionals; others engage in the non-professional, intermittent environment. Up and down Island in all seasons, even in the mud months of late winter/early spring, singers, instrumentalists, soloists and groups put themselves out there, entertaining, educating, appearing for fundraisers and expressing their virtuosities. On the Vineyard, not a season goes by without myriad forms of music, from Bach to the Beatles to the blues, served up to discriminating, appreciative audiences.

ACKNOWLEDGEMENTS

The authors discovered that pure gold nuggets are buried in Martha's Vineyard's musical past and present. A full range of musical genres is supported by a full set of infrastructure services: teaching by a renowned, now on-line pedagogue and dedicated public school teachers; global instrument repair by the repairman to the gods; the projection of music genes to many of today's budding talents; a wide variety of venues; recording and producing access for America's great musicians; generous and appreciative audiences; role models aplenty; a creative aura pervading the Island's atmosphere; and finally, a sense of tradition that calls forth the best in the Island's performers.

To all those associated with music on Martha's Vineyard, we thank you.

The Vineyard Sound is a body of water separating the Vineyard from Cape Cod and the Elizabeth Islands. The Vineyard Sound is also the name of a sparkling group of young men who entertain the Island each summer with marvelous a cappella singing. The Vineyard Sound is a recorded collection of songs, mostly with Island and beach themes, sung by several of the Island's best singers. The music that emanates from these musically gifted singers is what the authors mean by "the Vineyard sound."

For those who perform their music publicly, we thank you.

The gold nuggets were not hard to come by. The dozens of people we interviewed were delighted to share their knowledge, and the sources of information were, for the most part, plentiful. The authors don't claim that the coverage of the music of Martha's Vineyard in this book is exhaustive—merely that it is a comprehensive first attempt.

And to the newspapers and magazines, museums, libraries, radio stations and venues where music is performed, we thank you. We especially acknowledge the archival research of librarian Hilary Wall of the *Vineyard Gazette* (whose father played the banjo and the bagpipes) and photographs supplied by Dan Waters (who plays guitar to accompany his poetry). To Tabitha Dulla, Darcy Mahan and Dani McGrath of The History Press, we express our appreciation for your support in this endeavor. And to our dear wives, Joyce Dresser and Carol Muskin, we couldn't have done this without your encouragement.

Writing this book has been a labor of love—one that was pure joy in writing. See? The Island's aura has seduced us, too.

Chapter 1

TAKE IT FROM THE TOP

To understand the role of music and musicians on Martha's Vineyard is to study the Island's musical heritage, beginning with the earliest residents: the Wampanoags. Music is wrapped up in dance for the Wampanoags. Dance takes two forms: social dance is lively, with the beat of a hardwood stick, a water drum and corn rattles, while ceremonial dance is an expression of appreciation and gratitude. Wampanoag Ramona Peters said, "Part of our nature is to be in thanksgiving. It's sort of our philosophy, so it gets threaded through both the social and ceremonial dances."[1] Ancient traditions are replicated in the songs and dances on sacred sites on the Vineyard by the Wampanoag tribe of Gay Head/Aquinnah.

Woody Vanderhoop graduated from Dartmouth College, traveled for a couple years and then returned to his native Vineyard in 2000. He works with the Wampanoag tribe of Gay Head/Aquinnah. He said, "This is where I live. Good energy. Good spirit here."

In the 1980s, Woody Vanderhoop formed Black Brook Singers, a community drumming group in Gay Head, now Aquinnah. "A bunch of local kids on our own developed our own style," he says. "We were singing northern and southern songs. 'Northern' or 'southern' refers to the plains." Wampanoags sing in the eastern style. "We made our own songs, whatever one of us are [*sic*] feeling. We try to feel that energy."

The Black Brook Singers performed at the wedding of Jason Baird and Jessie Little Dove, in 2004, at the Vanderhoop homestead by the cliffs. "The Wampanoag Wedding Song," created specifically for that ceremony, was sung in the Wampanoag language. The words translate to mean: "Now you are taking care of each other. We are all happy. We will all remember this day." Woody is proud to be part of the tradition of this vibrant culture. With the renewal of the singing tradition, he says, "We are a living culture."[2]

The Black Brook drumming group performs across Martha's Vineyard. In 2012, members of the Wampanoag Tribe performed a drumming program for the Adult and Community Education (ACE) Cultural Festival. They beat a constant rhythm, with occasional quicker, louder beats, chanting to the beat. A young boy held his own. It was a steady drumming, occasioned by a firmer, then softer beat, with a constant flow of energy.[3]

From the singing and drumming of the Wampanoag, the Drum Workshop has earned its place, keeping the beat in Island music. "The Drum Workshop was developed in response to a request from the community," says founder Rick Bausman. In the late 1980s, a preschool teacher asked him to bring in his drums to let the children play. "I didn't want to have just a bunch of people making noise," Bausman said, "so I used it as a teachable experience. I came up with focused activities, like dynamics and tempo, and used imagery to play elephant or butterfly sounds." Preschoolers handled their drums well.

Bausman believes authentic rhythms enhance self-esteem more than random drum circles. "There's a lot to be said for learning specific parts and putting the parts together," he said. "You have to listen to other people, receive the support of other people; it's helpful for people on the Asperger's spectrum or [with] Parkinson's disease. It connects people." Playing traditional beats is a link with past generations. Bausman said, "You're connected to people who have done this for generation upon generation."

PROGRAMME

OF

MR. G. C. WHEELER'S

CONCERT!

APRIL 30th, 1875.

PART 1.

1. CONCERT OVERTURE.   *G. W. Stratton*
      Misses Olive and Lizzie Sturtevant.

2. SOLO. FROM NORMA.   *Bellini.*
      Miss Grace C. West.

3. PIANO SOLO. TRUST IN GOD. (Reply to the last hope.)   *Melnotte.*
      Miss Hepsie Nickerson.

4. DECLAMATION. SELECTED.
      Charlie Brown.

5. PIANO SOLO. TRANSCRIPTIONS. (Old Oaken Bucket.) *T. P. Ryder.*
      Miss Etta D. Cleavland.

6. SOLO. EBB AND FLOW.
      Miss Sarah Johnson.

7. RECITATION. (THE DYING SOLDIER.)
      Miss Olive Sturtevant.

8. PIANO SOLO. GRAND MARCH DE CONCERT.   *Melnotte.*
      Mr. G. C. Wheeler.

PART 2.

1. CONCERT OVERTURE. FRIA DI AVOLO.   *Auber.*
      Misses Nickerson and Johnson.

2. DUET. A GOLDEN DAY.   *Campana.*
      Misses West and Harding.

3. RECITATION. WHO SAVED ST. MICHAELS?
      Miss Etta D. Cleavland.

4. PIANO SOLO. SAILOR'S EVENING SONG, } *G. C. Wheeler.*
             STUDENT'S MARCH.
      By The Author.

5. PEGASUS GRAND GALLOP.   *Scheuman.*
      Misses Olive and Lizzie Sturtevant.

6. GOLDEN BELLS CAPRICE DE CONCERT.   *Sidney Smith.*
      Misses Lizzie Merry and Minnie Harding.

☞ The Piano used at this Concert is from the celebrated manufactory of HENRY F. MILLER, Boston, Mass.

Program from a piano concert with choral pieces on April 30, 1875. *Courtesy of the Martha's Vineyard Museum.*

In 1846, the first year of its publication, the editor of the *Vineyard Gazette* wrote about church music, saying, "Singing the praises of God is one of the most exalted employments that can possibly be engaged in by intelligent beings on earth or in heaven." The article described church music as an "enlivening part of worship" for the congregation and especially focused on the "harmony of feeling and of action among the members of a choir."

The newspaper article advocated singing as a "work of cultivation [that] should be commenced in childhood." Furthermore, "singers should not despise their own gifts and capacities for the work, nor those of any others who join with them."

The editor concluded, "Music itself has a power and a sweetness in it which, if allowed to blend with the better feelings of our nature, will have a strong tendency to exterminate petty jealousies and animosities from the breast, and soothe us to consonance and fellowship."[4] Music calms the soul and promotes those religious ideals advocated from the pulpit.

A piano arrived on the Vineyard in 1835. "It was to the home of a Vineyard captain that the first Island piano came,"[5] a Chickering and Mackay piano, #2161, shipped from Boston to the Vineyard on July 24. A second piano, #4869, arrived shortly thereafter, and a third ancient instrument is housed in the Martha's Vineyard Museum. The *Gazette* queried readers whether anyone knew of a piano older than 1835, as Nantucket claimed a piano had arrived there in 1831. This exemplifies the continuing competition between the two islands.

Music Street, in West Tisbury, was renamed after several whaling captains brought pianos home, which were played by their wives and daughters. Previously, the street had been called Cow Turd Lane.

In the days of slavery, a key element of music was information exchange. Today, a musical ensemble revives the virtues of singing in a spiritual choir. "The purpose of the [singing] project is to educate the general public on the history and interpretation of slave songs, spirituals," Jim Thomas said, explaining the goals of his U.S. Slave Spiritual Choir, organized in 2004. "Spirituals are a very early form of communication [and] social media."

The first slaves were teenagers who typically had a desire to communicate. They came from various tribes in Africa, where communication via song was common. Forbidden to speak to one another by their masters, the slaves sang their spirituals using a religious format. "The slaves used a safe language to communicate," says Thomas. "[There were] always at least two levels of messages in these songs: one, the obvious to the master, the other to the slaves. Until after the [Civil] War, no one wanted to believe the slaves were communicating a message." Words such as river, water and Jordan, for example, refer to the Middle Passage from Africa.

When singing "Go Down Moses," they were referring to Harriet Tubman, the escaped slave and abolitionist. "Another code [word] was angels, which appeared during the time of the documented Underground Railroad, from 1830 to 1860. Angels were conductors on the Underground Railroad, the underlying meaning of 'Swing Low Sweet Chariot.'"

Thomas says, "You can play the really old spirituals with only the black notes on the keyboard, the sharps and flats. From the top, going down, you get a flat, which introduces the first blue note—the blues, and jazz." Hence, we understand that it was from the slave songs and spirituals that the blues was born.

Chapter 2

ON THE SEA TO "BY THE SEA"

In 1951, the *Vineyard Gazette* stated, "The culture of the old days was inseparably bound up with the whaling industry." In an introduction to his popular 1964 tome, *Songs the Whalemen Sang*, Gale Huntington explained, "It was in the little towns on Nantucket and Martha's Vineyard, and about the shores of Buzzard's Bay that whaling became an established industry."[6]

"Music—song—was one of the very few real pleasures that whalemen had," wrote Huntington.[7] Songs celebrated triumph and tragedy aboard ship. Yet "the only songs that were not recorded in the journals are the chanties. And that is because the whalemen, like all seamen, did not think of the chanties as songs at all. They were a part of the routine of working ships and everyone knew them."[8] *Songs the Whalemen Sang* captured the musical tradition of the whaling industry.

Huntington's book was reprinted by Mystic Seaport in 2006 and reviewed by Mark Lovewell, the *Vineyard Gazette*'s maritime reporter. According to Lovewell, the book "remains a landmark work, preserving the melodies of a bygone era and also giving insight into the lives of the whalemen of the 1700s and 1800s."[9]

Music was a basic element in the work of the whalemen. When Herman Melville sailed aboard the whaleboat *Acushnet*, he recognized the value of singing. He wrote:

"I heard Gale Huntington and his wife, Mildred, sing duets in a coffeehouse," said Bob Hammond, of the Flying Elbows. *Courtesy of Mark Lovewell.*

> *I soon got used to this singing, for the sailors never touched a rope without it. Sometimes, the mate would always say, "Come men, can't any of you sing? Sing now and raise the dead." I am sure the song was well worth the breath expended on it. It is a great thing in a sailor to know how to sing well, for he gets a great name by it from the officers. Some sea captains, before shipping a man, always ask him whether he can sing out at a rope.*[10]

A majority of the songs in Huntington's book relate to work on whaling ships, from hauling a whale carcass aboard ship to hoisting a sail or raising an anchor. "The value of books like these does not diminish with age—they increase," said Lovewell, who continued, "The more this Island changes with the times, the more people ask about who was here before." *Songs the Whalemen Sang* treasures those years.[11]

Like the sailors who sang them, sea chanteys traveled from ship to ship for years before they were written down. Gale Huntington wrote, "And so the songs that the Vineyard people sang (before the days of the phonograph, radio or television) came from the forecastles and cabins of the ships of all nations on which Vineyard men sailed. They are a part of the heritage of the Island."[12]

Troubadour Mark Lovewell has assumed the legacy of Gale Huntington, the sea chantey enthusiast and authority. Lovewell is the link between whaling music and the modern era. Lovewell met and befriended Gale and Mildred Huntington. Gale told him, "Sing sea chanteys. No one else is doing it.'"

Mark Lovewell says, "One of the greatest gifts that came along was that people encourage you." He goes on, primarily focusing on Gale Huntington. "People in my life are huge. They want me to tell stories and sing songs about the maritime." He says his creative energy is encouraged by positive responses from those around him.

Poet Dionis Coffin Riggs performed with Mark and encouraged him to give his songs context. She read her poems, and he sang and told tales. They were fifty years apart in age, yet that made it all the better. "They were delightful," recalls Cynthia Riggs, Dionis's daughter.

Mark Lovewell, pictured aboard his *Sea Chantey*, says, "A child growing up in an environment surrounded by an appreciation for music, for the maritime, for the Vineyard, is living your childhood dream." *Courtesy of Mark Lovewell.*

Photographer Mark Lovewell plays the concertina. His great-grandmother Anna, a piano player, married a piano manufacturer, Julian Vose. *Courtesy of Mark Lovewell.*

"I've always had a love of the ocean, for the poetry of the ocean," Mark Lovewell says, and his face grows animated. "Imagine a child coming to the Vineyard in the summer, loving the sea. It was a gradual transition, it was an evolution, building blocks; it's not a line in the sand, but I can say I knew these songs as a teenager." Lovewell's enthusiasm is contagious.

Mark Lovewell's favorite sea chantey is "Rolling Home." "Every time I close a concert, I sing that song. It is sentimental and has universal appeal. I always talk about whaling, coming home, maritime history and the community of Martha's Vineyard."

The lyrics were uncovered by unusual means, confides Lovewell: "Only divulged when Alton Tilton was drunk." He explains, "Emily, a little child, wants to give her father, Gale, something special as a birthday present. So Emily got him [Alton Tilton] drunk, and got the words to the song ['Rolling Home'] and gave them to her father."

The Vineyard Haven Band lays claim to being the oldest continuous musical assemblage on Martha's Vineyard. The band's early history consists of hazy memories, as all band records, music and instruments burned in a fire at the Christ Methodist Church in Vineyard Haven in 1922. With the loss of documentation, our story depends on memories passed by word of mouth, from trumpet player to clarinetist, from father to son.[13]

The band arose from shards of the Civil War. According to the Vineyard Haven Band website, "In 1868, eighteen Civil War veterans (both blue and gray) organized the Vineyard Haven Silver Cornet Brass Band in order to play at the West Tisbury Agricultural Association Fair, and also to earn side money by playing for socials."[14]

The band performed for the president of the United States in the late summer of 1874, when Ulysses S. Grant visited Oak Bluffs. Francis Vincent Pease[15] was a member of a prominent Vineyard family and conducted the band for nearly forty years. Pease served as bugler and as dispatch rider for General Grant, so the president knew him. "One of the conditions President Grant set out," reported band historian Tom Bardwell, "was for Frances Pease to put together a crackerjack band. Grant knew Pease had background with band experience."

The Vineyard Haven Band is pictured in 1899. The Vineyard Haven Silver Cornet Band was renamed the Vineyard Haven Brass Band in 1883, and the name was abbreviated to the Vineyard Haven Band in 1919. Woodwinds and women were not welcome. *Courtesy of Chris Baer.*

The Nobnocket Orchestra consisted of Alton Tuckerman, Fred Peakes and S.C. Luce Jr., pictured circa 1915. *Courtesy of Chris Baer.*

In preparation for the president, the town fathers had a bandstand constructed in Ocean Park. This gazebo stands today as a symbol of when the president came to town. Children adorned in white toted flags around the gazebo as the band played. That tradition of children marching around the gazebo continues to this day, reminding the audience of a Norman Rockwell painting, a real piece of Americana.

President Grant's visit was highlighted by a "grand procession" from the campground to Dr. Tucker's house in Ocean Park. That evening, at the house of Bishop Haven, President Grant was serenaded and "bade goodnight to the quartet that sang below his balcony." This presidential visit foretold such visits for the future.[16]

The band marched in Memorial Day parades and, in the mid-1890s, initiated Sunday evening concerts in Vineyard Haven and Oak Bluffs.

Another aspect of the Sunday evening band concerts was the publicity surrounding Oak Bluffs as a popular vacation site toward the end of the nineteenth century. Besides the band, tourists flocked to Cottage City, as the town was known, to stroll along the shore, ride the carousel and savor the seaside sights. "Oak Bluffs was being touted as a 'Great American Watering Place,' as attractive and fashionable a resort as Long Branch in New Jersey, Saratoga, or Newport. It gave the language a new idiom, for example, 'bluffing' came to mean the ever-popular moonlight stroll out to Lover's Rock. Bands played a song called the Oak Bluffs Galop [sic]. The tune probably moved to a faster beat than did the couples who went bluffing."[17] Little is known of Etta Godrey, who composed the Oak Bluffs Galop in 1872.

The Flying Horses carousel was featured in a July 9, 1886 *Vineyard Gazette* advertisement, which announced that there was "fun for the old folks as well as for the children at the horse carousel on the Bluffs." The owner boasted that the facility was lit by electricity and offered "Good Music." The *Gazette* observed, "One of the most entertaining places of the resort at Cottage City is the 'Carousel.' The large airy building, with its broadside open to the sea, the flying horses, and the inspiring music proving almost equally attractive to young and old."

One visitor was so moved by the ambiance of the seaside site that he wrote a song that he dedicated to the people of Martha's Vineyard. In 1915, Thomas J. Ryan composed "Dear Old Martha's Vineyard."[18]

Will Hardy played piano with his six-piece orchestra. The Tivoli (pictured) became the center of musical enjoyment on the Vineyard. *Courtesy of the Martha's Vineyard Museum.*

Arthur Railton wrote, in his definitive *History of Martha's Vineyard*, "It was a rare evening when the sound of fox trots didn't fill the evening air." "Tivoli Girl" was a popular tune played at the Tivoli. *Courtesy of Martha's Vineyard Museum.*

"Tivoli Girl" sheet music by Will Hardy, 1917. *Courtesy of the Martha's Vineyard Museum.*

There's a place called Martha's Vineyard
It's an island out at sea
And of all the spots upon this earth
'Tis heaven above to me:
'Twas the birthplace of my father and
My mother dear, as well,
How much I love this dear old isle
No tongue on earth can tell.

The hub of summer activity in Oak Bluffs was the Tivoli, which opened in 1907. By 1916, it gained prominence "when Will Hardy brought his Novelty Orchestra from Worcester. It was a magnet, attracting not only summer people, but year-round Islanders as well."[19]

Easily identified by two towers, one at either end, the Tivoli was a large wooden structure, painted yellow. The second-floor ballroom opened up onto a wide veranda, which allowed dance music to flow outside.

In the 1920s, groups of musicians played jazz, with improvisation by trumpets, trombones or clarinets. Each instrument had a defined role, but the music was improvised. Arrangements for swing focused on an intense rhythm with repeated riffs. Soloists would be featured, with the rhythm section providing the beat. Improvisation allowed musicians an artistic freedom of self-expression.

Swing was the style of jazz popular in the 1930s, the era of big bands in dance halls or music furnished by a radio or records. Freedom and abandon in the improvisational musical style offered a release and an escape from the anguish and suffering of the Great Depression.

At the Tivoli, "live music was furnished by visiting dance bands," wrote Stuart MacMackin in 1983. No liquor was served, but a soda fountain and souvenir shops were on the lower level.[20]

"In the 1930s some of the nation's best-known dance bands entertained in brief stands on weekends, but it was Will Hardy's sextet that created the magic of the Tivoli. You didn't have to dance to feel the Tivoli magic. Thousands were enthralled by the music as they strolled along Circuit Avenue."[21] Band leader and composer Will Hardy ran the Tivoli ballroom from 1915 to 1931. Hardy's "endearing, all-time favorite 'Tivoli Girl' (1917)" is evocative of the era.[22]

The Tivoli was demolished in 1964 for the Oak Bluffs Town Hall, now the police headquarters.

Chapter 3

A SONG-AND-DANCE ERA

While people flocked to the Tivoli in Oak Bluffs or listened to the band play in Vineyard Haven, the locals up-Island conducted their own musical medleys. One family in particular, the Tiltons, earned an Island-wide reputation for their singing prowess.

"The Singing Tiltons (and that's what they were called) were proud of their heritage and known Island-wide, and even beyond the Island, for their songs." As an extensive Vineyard family, "they were known as the North Road Tiltons to distinguish them from the Middle Road Tiltons, the South Road Tiltons, and the down-Island Tiltons."[23]

Seven Tilton sons and a daughter, Flora, made up the progeny of George Oliver and Hannah Tilton. All seven sons loved to sing. The story goes that when they were growing up, "a Tilton would wake up some time in the middle of the night, and if he felt like singing he'd sing. Pretty soon the fire would be built up on the hearth again and all the family would be gathered by it singing. That's the sort of reputation they had."[24]

The eldest Tilton, William (1854–1941), "following his innate talents, took to ditty singing."[25] Of Welcome Tilton (1856–1949), Huntington wrote, "Since he was my wife's grandfather, he is the one I had the most contact with and learned the most songs from."[26]

Edward Van Buren Tilton (1858–1920) "never did anything but sing Gospel if he could help it. He was known as the 'Chilmark Singer' at every isolated farm on Martha's Vineyard, Cape Cod and Nantucket.

He could often be seen walking from Gay Head, where he might have visited some Indian friends, to Vineyard Haven, some twenty miles distant, singing all the way." Van Buren visited his neighbors, sharing his songs and news of the Island in exchange for a meal and a place to spend the night.[27]

Of the remaining Tiltons, George Fred Tilton (1860–1932) was not very musically inclined, and Zebulon Tilton (1866–1952) was better known for his coasting schooner, the *Alice B. Wentworth*, than his singing. Gale Huntington never knew John Tilton, except that he sang well, and Willard Earl, the youngest, "was a fine singer, but he lived in Edgartown and I only saw him occasionally."[28]

As Gale Huntington recalled, "Artie Look and I, with Hollis Smith, another fiddle player, were the square dance team on the Island at that time. He [Look] was a tremendous natural musician and I learned most of my best fiddle tunes from him. We played for square dances all over the Island."[29] Their musical heritage began one evening in 1928, when Artie and Gale learned that "Welcome wants to have a musical time."[30]

Over the years, Gale Huntington listened, learned and transcribed dozens of folksongs sung by the Tiltons. One of the songs Bill Tilton sang was "Brave Boys," also known as "The Greenland Whale," a popular nineteenth-century whaling song that speaks to the economic value of whaling and the dangers involved.

> *When the captain he heard of the loss of his men*
> *It grieved his heart full sore.*
> *But when he heard of the loss of that whale,*
> *Why it grieved him ten times more, brave boys,*
> *It grieved him ten times more.*

In his book *Folksongs from Martha's Vineyard*, Gale Huntington refers to Welcome Tilton and his songs, saying, "Looking back it seems as though there was much more singing in the old days than there is now. And one thing is sure, the singing then was much less self-conscious. Another thing, people don't whistle the way they used to…I don't know what has brought about these changes but it would be very easy to blame radio and television."[31]

In the first half of the twentieth century, Harry T. Burleigh (1866–1949) was a frequent guest at Shearer Cottage in Oak Bluffs, an inn that catered to African Americans denied access in other hotels. Burleigh was instrumental in encouraging African Americans from New York to visit the Vineyard. He was a baritone, a classical composer, an arranger and a soloist. His musical legend lives on in his collection of Negro spirituals entitled *Jubilee Songs of the United States of America*. According to a website about Harry T. Burleigh's work, "He popularized the spirituals and showed the world their great power and beauty. He bridged cultures and races by using the inspiring songs of his ancestors."

One of Burleigh's teachers, Antonin Dvorak, asked his assistance in his own symphony, *From the New World*. Dvorak was intrigued by the songs Burleigh had learned from his grandfather, a blind slave. Teacher and student became close, and Dvorak urged Burleigh to pursue artistic arrangements of the spirituals, which made them accessible to the public.

Another Shearer Cottage guest was Lillian Evanti (1890–1967), "acclaimed as the first African American female professional opera singer," according to the Shearer Cottage website. A soprano, Lillian Evanti sang with Marian Anderson in 1926. Miss Evanti was the first African American classical singer to perform grand opera.

While Burleigh promoted African American spirituals, the Vineyard Haven Band was busy offering marching music to the Island community. Alton Tuckerman recalled that the Vineyard Haven Band would play three concerts a day for three days at the Agricultural Fair in the early twentieth century. Tuckerman, a plumber, could play "any kind of horn that may be desired but [he stuck] fairly consistently to the largest and most crooked horn in the group." Tuckerman played in the band for half a century, retiring in the 1950s.

In 1942, at the beginning of World War II, Edgartown's Fourth of July parade "start[ed] on the dot of 10 o'clock." The Vineyard Haven Band and the Oak Bluffs Bugle and Drum Corps marched. That night, the band performed at 7:30 p.m. in Owen Park. The concert began a half hour earlier than usual to accommodate wartime blackout regulations. On July 5, "a patriotic parade, designed to demonstrate just what the town is doing to aid in national defense" would be held in Oak Bluffs, wrote the *Vineyard Gazette* on July 3, with another concert at Ocean Park.

Later that year, on November 20, the *Vineyard Gazette* observed, "This is supposed to be an age of swing and all that, but when the boys in uniform harmonize they seem well content with 'My Wild Irish Rose' which was used to beguile comparable moments back in 1917 and 1918. Possibly you cannot set war, or mankind at war, to new kinds of music."

The Vineyard Haven Band continued to entertain large audiences throughout the Second World War. A good-sized crowd gathered to hear the band play at Ocean Park in the summer of 1943, but automobiles "were conspicuous by their absence," due to tire and gas rationing and pleasure-driving restrictions during the war. Nevertheless, "the music was most satisfactory and heartily applauded."[32]

The United Service Organization (USO) provided entertainment for servicemen during the war. Fundraisers were held to support the USO, and actress Katharine "Kit" Cornell headlined one such event at the Tisbury School in 1942.

The *Vineyard Gazette* noted, "Of course Miss Cornell will be right there, the Martha's Vineyard Miss Cornell, and it is noised about that she may sing a song, which is something she has not yet done on the stage." Nancy Hamilton, lyricist and partner of Katharine Cornell, performed, as did Miss Cornell's husband, Guthrie McClintic. Also on stage was Academy Award–winning actor Gregory Peck. And yes, Katharine Cornell did sing on stage. Kit Cornell's Jamboree raised over $1,500 for the USO.

School groups were active during the war years; both the Tisbury and Edgartown school orchestras presented concerts. Three trumpeters in the Tisbury orchestra were Gary Mosher, Lester Baptiste and George Luce; a pianist and xylophonist rounded out the group.[33]

When the Tisbury School Orchestra performed, "five hundred music fans, or more shook the Tisbury school auditorium with their applause at the winter concert."[34] Basketball games between servicemen were held at the Tisbury High gym. The *Vineyard Gazette* reported on January 14, 1944, "The games were followed by danced-to music supplied by records. The crowd was one of the largest of the season." And throughout the war, the Tivoli was "operated during the summer, for dancing, six nights a week, with name bands supplying the music."[35]

When the Tisbury School Orchestra, pictured here circa 1944, played to raise money for new uniforms, the *Vineyard Gazette* reported that the orchestra was "greeted with enthusiasm and rewarded by a gratifying collection." *Courtesy of Martha Child.*

Those who enjoyed Cape Verdean music had a site to appreciate it. Joseph Stiles, interviewed in 2002, recalls attending

> *the dances they used to have at the Cape Verdean Hall when I was stationed on the Island during the War. We never missed one of them. All the sailors used to go. We never had to pay to go in, just walk in and start dancing and enjoying yourself. People would come from New Bedford. Jimmy Lomberg and his orchestra used to come over here; they'd play all Cape Verdean music. Their dances are like a reel. You don't get in the middle of the floor and just drag around. You'd be dancing like mad, but you'd be going in a circle so nobody would be bumping into each other.*

The dance hall was on Lake Street, Vineyard Haven.

A number of people of Cape Verdean and Azorean descent trace their ancestry back to the whaling days, when whale ships would stop in the Cape Verdean islands or the Azores to sign up more crew. Nantucket and

Through the years, many program directors have led the choir in song.
Courtesy of the Martha's Vineyard Museum.

New Bedford were known for being home harbor for whaling ships; Martha's Vineyard was known for providing more crew members. The communities are enriched by the Cape Verdeans who stayed, as well as by their music.

And for those who enjoy singing in general, the Tabernacle hosted Community Sings, a program that continues seasonally to this day. The Community Sings at the Tabernacle, "where people young and old gather to sing favorite songs and hymns, were mentioned as early as 1919," according to Sally Dagnall, campground historian. Miriam Williamson recalled, "Singing could be heard almost anywhere, almost anytime in Oak Bluffs because half the members of the choir of the Tabernacle lived together, played together and loved to sing together wherever they were."

Community Sings are still held on Wednesday evenings, with the Tabernacle bursting with hundreds of people. The Vineyard Haven Band prepares all season to perform on Illumination Night. The end-of-the-season concert in 1943 included songs such as "My Wild Irish Rose," "Keep the Home Fires Burning," "In the Gloaming" and Negro spirituals "Goin' to Shout," "Travlin' to a Grave" and "Oh, When I Get to Heaven."[36]

Chapter 4
A MUSICAL HIGH NOTE

The list of notable musicians who have spent significant time on the Vineyard is extensive. Some come to play gigs and move on; others stay to write and perform. Name-dropping is easy, and we will certainly do that. Musical luminaries express varied reasons for coming to the Vineyard. Our effort is directed at understanding the compelling allure of the Island. Perhaps Euterpe, the muse of music, has taken up residence on the Vineyard.

The 1920s in America brought postwar prosperity, along with both soothing and frenetic music (think the Charleston and the fox trot). It also brought the Dust Bowl and then the Depression. Out of these tragedies came the union movement and some liberals' interest in the populist principles of Communism.

Thomas Hart Benton (1889–1975) was a great American painter and muralist of the twentieth century. Celebrated on the Vineyard as a successful artist, he lived a bohemian lifestyle in Chilmark. His friendship circle included Max Eastman, the leftist editor; Roger Baldwin, the American Civil Liberties Union founder; and others in the radical intellectual crowd who frequented the cooperative Chilmark summer camp known as Barn House. Benton and Jimmy Cagney were close friends.

Benton believed the essence of America was inherent in the folk music of the hills and valleys of south-central United States. He feared that this unique music was in jeopardy of commercialization. He set about to visit the backcountry and, while sketching the performers, wrote down and recorded their music. His commitment to this mission, he claimed, arose from insight developed from the aura he encountered early in his life on Martha's Vineyard, where he summered from 1920 until his death in 1975.

In Annett Claudia Richter's book on Benton, she notes, "Not only did Benton preserve a considerable amount of America's musical heritage, but his collection is also valuable to musicologists with respect to the particular versions Benton documented in it."[37] One collection yielded 120 neatly copied folk songs, with piano accompaniment and numbers for each melodic pitch to get the right hole in his harmonica. (In 1931, Benton had discovered the mouth organ through his son, bought an instruction booklet for a dime and became a harmonica man. By the mid-1930s, Tom Benton and His Harmonica Boys proved popular.)

Benton explored his birthplace, the Ozarks, as well as the Appalachian and Blue Ridge Mountains. Richter explains, "His scholarly approach to the music of the regions justifies his being characterized as a musicologist and a folklorist."

Vineyard summers yielded friendships that produced classical and folk music. The group of music makers included Benton's Italian immigrant wife, Rita Piacenza, who played piano and guitar, and later, their son, Thomas Piacenza, a schooled and gifted flutist, along with musically talented locals. "Vineyarders kept the island's musical heritage alive by gathering for 'musical times' to sing old whaling and coasting songs after a day's work was done,"[38] and the Benton family took part in this tradition.

The Bentons' social life in Chilmark centered on music. Dances at the town hall were enlivened by a three-piece orchestra or a gramophone. Gale Huntington, Ernest and Wesley Correllus, Hollis Smith and Mike Athearn sang and played, as did actors Ed McNamara and James Cagney. An iconic image of the era "gives us the sense of the spontaneous and arbitrary mixture of both folk and classical music instruments played at these gatherings, depending on what musicians came."[39]

As Dr. Richter wrote, Thomas Hart Benton was "a remarkable folklorist whose ties to American folk music have long been overlooked by music historians…the artist captured performance practices of American folk music and produced visual images of the very musicians who shaped the folk music scene in rural America." Benton died in 1975 while completing his final mural, *The Sources of Country Music*, for the Country Music Hall of Fame in Nashville. Benton's social vision drove his music and his visual art.

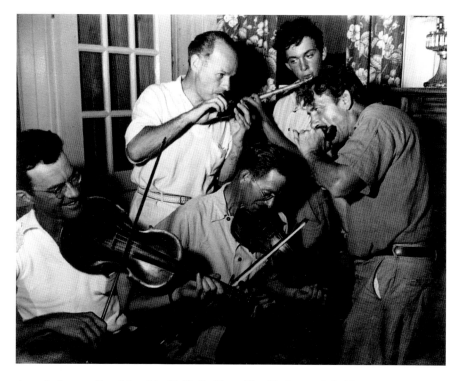

A musical event. *From left to right*: Hollis Smith, unidentified man, Gale Huntington, Thomas Piacenza Benton and Thomas Hart Benton. *Photo by Arthur C. Griffin, courtesy of the Martha's Vineyard Museum; photograph used with permission.*

The three—Woody Guthrie (1912–1967), Pete Seeger (1919–2014) and Benton—brought folk music back on the shoulders of what each saw as cultural injustice. They traveled, wrote, performed, shared Martha's Vineyard and admired one another. Richter writes, "We know that Benton also influenced Pete Seeger, in his early pursuits in folk music by teaching him folks songs on the harmonica at the Bentons' musical evenings in 1932."[40]

Seeger, later in life, pursued a mission of cleaning up the Hudson River. He named his sailboat the *Woody*, in honor of Woody Guthrie, and it was used in pursuit of his goal. The three—Benton, Seeger and Guthrie—revived the music of the common man: folk music. At one point, Seeger and his group, the Almanac Singers, recorded albums entitled *Deep Sea Chanties* and *Sod Buster Ballads*, returning folk music to its American roots of subsistence farming and the sea.

From the Depression through the 1950s and beyond, these passionate musical missionaries of social progress and social justice enlisted the youth of America in an awareness campaign about the national failures of unemployment, civil rights, preservation of the environment and international enmity. The movement expanded across a youthful audience and crossed a generational divide. The three musicians sought to save the soul of America; this precipitated the folk music explosion of the '50s and '60s and foretold the arrival of rock-and-roll, folk rock and, most notably, as far as the Vineyard was concerned, the singer/songwriter era.

The singer/songwriter movement flourished as audiences responded favorably to singers who sincerely implored listeners to be sensitive to their own needs and those of others. They wrote their own songs. It was a move beyond the coffeehouses of the era and encouraged the "open mic" phenomenon. The Island's Wintertide nurtured this movement by inviting accomplished musicians to perform along with those who were "on their way."

The primary development of the singer/songwriter phenomenon was on the "left coast," i.e., California. The Vineyard's James Taylor was a principal innovator/practitioner, holding forth at the Los Angeles venue the Troubadour. While singer/songwriters captivated large audiences of the younger generations, Pete Seeger and fellow folksingers continued to promote the environmental, peace and civil rights messages to audiences of all ages.

Burl Ives (1909–1995) was another luminous creator of folk music, one whose involvement was founded in much the same background as those of Thomas Hart Benton and Woody Guthrie. Like Guthrie, Ives came of age in the Depression, grew up on a poor family farm and traveled as an itinerant singer in the States and Mexico. The music he created and performed was not, in general, of the protest type. It was traditional, entertaining, instructive and popular with a very wide audience.

Ives sang country, songs of the British Isles, children's songs and, given his love of boats and the water, songs of the sea. He did play in a pro-war folk group early in World War II and was with a group that included Woody Guthrie and Pete Seeger that sang, largely, protest songs.

It is of note that Burl Ives taught at the West Chop School of Creative Arts in the early 1950s. The curriculum included art, dance, drama and music, and Ives sang folk songs with the students. Merce Cunningham led the dance program at the school, and Lotte Lenya, of "Mack the Knife" fame, led the singing.

Local troubadour Mark Lovewell, who was too young to have observed Ives's activities, says Burl Ives came to Edgartown on his boat: "I somehow heard that his visit[s] to Edgartown were a positive thing. It did set the tone for my own interest in folk music. We all felt good about what he did as a performing musician. Many loved the man, his voice, and the songs he sang."

An Oak Bluffs site known for liquid refreshment is the Lampost. Proprietor Ed Krickorian recalled one guest: "We had Burl Ives singing in there. Every summer Burl Ives used to come down here. I never seen a man eat so much popcorn in my life, but that's all right. He'd have a few drinks and he'd get up and sing. And everybody would sing along with him. It was a really happy hour, it was pretty good."[41]

Jimmy Cagney (1899–1986), the quintessential "song-and-dance man," was nominated for three Academy Awards and received one in 1943 for his lead in *Yankee Doodle Dandy*. His singing and dancing were legendary.

Cagney bought a two-hundred-acre farm with a modest house in the relaxed town of Chilmark and spent as much time as possible there between movies. Once a movie was "in the can," he'd hop a sleeper train from Hollywood. Early on, however, he encountered what he considered rejection by the locals, prompting him to write a rhyme.

> *When you give your heart to fair Martha's Isle*
> *That Queen of insular sluts*
> *It's like falling in love with a beautiful whore*
> *Who hates your goddamned guts.*

Cagney did eventually win over the locals and developed many friendships. The residents recognized his warmth and humanity and protected him from intrusions on his privacy by giving phony directions or feigning ignorance to tourists.

In his autobiography, *Cagney by Cagney*, he wrote, "I couldn't think of anything more satisfying than living on a farm surrounded by water. That's what Martha's Vineyard allowed me to do. I loved it beyond words." He enjoying taking actress Katharine Cornell sailing and became part of the left-leaning Barn House commune.

One day, the story goes, Cagney's boat was headed out on a sail, and his skipper asked Cagney where he'd like to go. Frank Sinatra was on the Vineyard in one-hundred-foot chartered yacht. The Island was atwitter. Sinatra was trying to contact Cagney. Jimmy's response to his skipper reportedly was "wherever Frank isn't."

Cagney bought more land and a house in upscale Edgartown, reflecting his love of the Island. Yet old friends were dying off, and his ability to enjoy the Island was shrinking. He moved ashore.

The tenure of Leonard Bernstein (1918–1990) on the Island offers a point of interest. Bernstein escaped the pressures of myriad intrusions on his time by moving to the Vineyard to work with his team on Voltaire's *Candide* in 1953. This version of *Candide* was his and playwright Lillian Hellman's satirical shot at the ongoing McCarthy hearings. (Voltaire's 1758 novella satirized the Catholic Church.) At his Island house, Bernstein, Hellman and Broadway director Tyrone Guthrie brought *Candide* to stage readiness. The show opened at the end of 1956 to mixed reviews.

During Bernstein's time on the Vineyard, the British playwright/composer Noel Coward came to dinner. That evening, he played songs he had written for a new show, *Sail Away*, for which Bernstein reportedly rendered an ambiguous critique. Another account, related by Bernstein, was Coward's walking off with Bernstein's silk kimono, which he had recently brought back from Japan. It seems Lenny wore it to dinner. Coward, admiring its silken beauty, asked to try it on. Bernstein claimed he never saw it again.

Eddie Heywood (1915–1989) was a popular jazz pianist and composer associated with pop and jazz musicians from the 1940s through the '70s. He became a year-round Vineyarder in 1962. *People* magazine introduced Mr. Heywood in a 1975 piece entitled "Eddie Heywood Sets the Vineyard to Music." The article noted, "The first time Eddie Heywood set foot on the Island he turned around and went back to the mainland on the next ferry. 'I'm not living any place I can't leave when I want to,' he said. But now he doesn't want to leave."

The *People* piece noted, "He was moved to compose the Martha's Vineyard Suite, an interpretation of the Island's changing seasons. For the Bicentennial, Heywood, 59, is recording a *Portrait of American Music*. A musical tour of our country, it includes such stopovers as St. Louis Blues, Sutton Place, Nob Hill and, of course, the Vineyard."

Heywood was a man of music, devoted to the Island. When Cole Porter heard Heywood play "Begin the Beguine," Porter said, "I wish that I'd composed this the way that you play it." He added, "You're a born composer." Inspired, Heywood overcame physical ailments of partial paralysis and Parkinson's and returned to composing.

Heywood's obituary cited a series of successes, including "Soft Summer Breeze" and "Canadian Sunset," which enabled him to settle on Martha's Vineyard. On the Island, he composed more than forty songs, including "Portrait of Martha's Vineyard," a tone poem.[42]

In 1957, folksinger Gale Huntington (1902–1993) recorded an album entitled *Folksongs from Martha's Vineyard*. Huntington, a square dance fiddler, included the popular contradance "Pop Goes the Weasel," and other folk tunes such as "Scarlet Town," "Blow the Man Down," "Gunpowder Tea" and "The Old Arm Chair." The latter had passed through the generations from Zeb Tilton to Gale Huntington and was later recorded by Mark Lovewell.

As Huntington researched American folk songs, an archivist from the Folk Music Division of the Library of Congress visited him. The *Vineyard Gazette* reported on June 15, 1973, "They taped old-time Vineyard fiddle tunes played by Mr. Huntington and Hollis Smith, who were backed-up on the guitar by Mr. Huntington's daughter [Emily]."

Mark Lovewell has assimilated many folk songs researched by Gale Huntington, just as he has the sea chanteys. "I've had an affection for folk music since high school," Lovewell says. His grandmother advised him that he could not make money as a folk singer. Nor as a writer. Nor a photographer. "So I do all three," says Lovewell, gleefully. "I'm making a living. You do multiple things to get through. It's a Vineyard way."

Mark Lovewell promotes the legacy of folksongs. He says, "Somebody on Martha's Vineyard needs to share these songs. The story of Martha's Vineyard is an amazing story; [you] can't just tuck it away in books." Lovewell plays and sings across the Vineyard and beyond. In 2013, he performed before 1,800 people in forty concerts, singing sea chanteys and telling stories. His CDs preserve the tales and tunes of bygone days.

"I played at George Monroe's Boston House," recalls Gene Baer. "Three big rooms, and I was the only entertainment. Summertime was a good time for piano players. They paid me, and tips, too." Gene Baer was a piano journeyman, who played at various Vineyard venues from the 1950s on. He said, "Basically, I played whatever I knew. Most people probably thought I was a college boy working my way through school."

The Boston House was on Circuit Avenue in Oak Bluffs, where the Game Room is now. Gene Baer played piano in the bar. He remembers, "It was a very popular drinking hole and kept a number of bartenders busy. Great clientele. All kinds of people in there." The Boston House "was a place, back then, in my mind, one of the few places on island where black people were welcome. It was a big meeting place between blacks and whites. You knew they felt at home. This was their place as much as anyone's place."

Gene Baer was not a trained musician: "I played what I could play. [When I didn't know a song,] I used a 'fake book,' which gave the melody and the chords of what to play up above."

He continued, "Leonard Bernstein used to come over on a Sunday afternoon and would sit down next to the piano and have a drink. He sat with me, and we talked. And then people began to pay more attention to my playing. His word carried such influence that others listened to him."

Another celebrity dropped by. "I'm absolutely positive this happened," says Baer. "A wealthy black man took me aside to introduce me to a man who has many names. I'm sure he was Nat King Cole. We befriended each other."

"The other place I played a long time was the Ritz. The Ritz always had a bad name, but it wasn't a bad place. Basically it was the workingman's bar. Men and women would dress up and go upstairs and dance on the upper deck. We played dance [music] and swing," he recalls. "There were people in there, unbelievable characters, people from all walks of life. It was wild but never any real trouble."

Shirley Mayhew also fondly recalls her early days on the Vineyard: "I remember the 1950s as a good decade—the war was over and I had happily settled in West Tisbury on an island I had never heard of before I met and married Johnny Mayhew, who was a descendent of a long line of Vineyarders."[43]

Back then, after Labor Day, local restaurants and movie theaters closed for the season. "So it was up to us to make our own fun. And we got together to play music," Mayhew said. Families gathered, with the men making music and women and children listening.

"Everett Whiting and Johnny [Mayhew] played guitar and Willie Huntington was good on the guitar as well as the banjo. Mike Athearn was the only accordion player, and Jack Scannell tried hard to mix in with a kazoo. Ernest Correllus and Elmer Silva occasionally joined us," according to Mayhew, who remembers that time as if it were yesterday. "They all played and sang old favorites, some not fit for children to hear, but it was our only entertainment and we enjoyed it."

Children of the several families followed family tradition: "The music got into the Huntington boys, as well as into my family. My son Jack and my daughter Deborah play the guitar and Deborah has handed down her lovely voice to her daughter, Katie Ann. Jack's two grown daughters are both accomplished musicians."

Shirley's granddaughter Katie Ann Mayhew earned a stellar reputation as a singer while still in her teens. Besides excelling in the high school Minnesingers, she won a statewide music contest and, as winner,

The Bodes are pictured in 1966. "Jack Mayhew was in a high school band called the Bodes, and even after some forty-five years, they still get together for an occasional gig," recalls Shirley Mayhew of her son Jack and his band. *Courtesy of Shirley Mayhew for Martha's Vineyard Magazine.*

was invited to sing at Boston's Fourth of July Esplanade concert and has ventured both to the West Coast and to London to sing.

Shirley Mayhew continues: "The first fair I attended was in 1946, and I haven't missed one since." A popular summer gathering place was the Agricultural Fair, originally held at the Grange Hall. "Willie and his brother, Gale Huntington, along with Elmer Silva and Ernest Correllus and others, sat on the front porch of the Grange Hall with their banjos and guitars and provided music for the annual event."

As recently as 2011, Shirley and her husband, Johnny, attended the fair "specifically to listen to a performance of the Flying Elbows, because my granddaughter Caroline was joining them with her fiddle for a few songs." She adds, "It was a sweet moment, and I was almost overwhelmed with nostalgia when I realized I was able to listen to the third generation of local musicians, and what a wonderful tradition had been started more than fifty years ago here in West Tisbury."

Shirley Mayhew added, "Jimmy Athearn plays the trombone in a swing orchestra which played forties music at Johnny's and my fortieth wedding anniversary party. Well, that was our era of music. These boys all grew up together."

Kate Taylor, James Taylor's sister, recalled her family's involvement in the Vineyard music scene. "Back in the early '50s our family started visiting the Vineyard in the summertime. Early on, the Chilmark Community Center became the epicenter for our summer activities. Colin Upson would host community sings. He'd play guitar and we'd all sing along. There were square dances every week and this was the basis for our social life. In later years Colin would invite some of us summer folks to perform. Before the Chilmark Community Center was built, the action in Chilmark was at the Tavern. These days there is a restaurant there, called The Tavern, giving a nod to the earlier incarnation."[44]

Chapter 5

A GOLDEN ERA

Dave Seward of Vineyard Haven recalled a landmark concert in the early '60s: "We got wind of a pick up concert at the Chilmark Tavern. In this 1962 concert we heard Tom Rush, Bill Keith and Carly Simon. It was an amazing concert. John Rogers recorded it; my brother has a copy of it. That was the beginning of folk music on Martha's Vineyard."[45]

Kate Taylor was at the Chilmark Tavern as well: "Back in the beginning of the '60s, someone was still presenting concerts in there. One summer night, when I was about 13, I went with some of my pals to hear Tom Rush and Davey Gude. It was very exciting for us, as we were already somewhat familiar with Tom's great song choices and rusty baritone and we weren't too young to be fans. I had four brothers and no sisters and when he introduced the song 'I Wish I Could Shimmy Like My Sister Kate,' I was thrilled and I let out a shriek."

She adds to the tale:

> *I took on the moniker of Sister Kate, and in fact 6 or 7 years later, that was the name I gave to my first record album.*
>
> *Almost 50 years later my friends Andy Palmer and Annie Eddy were asking me whether I knew if there was a way to re-record old acetate recordings and filter out all the pops and hisses that get on these things with age and use. I said I knew it was possible now with the new technologies, and asked what was the recording they had? They said it*

The Moon Cusser coffeehouse was a place where people "could feed their growing interest in folk music, listening to some of the best folk and blues musicians of the time," recalled manager David Lyman. *Courtesy of David Lyman.*

was an acetate that was cut at the Tavern the night of the Tom Rush show way back when. I came over to their house to have a listen, and it sounded great in spite of all the cracks and pops. And when it came to the place on the disc where Tom Rush was introducing "I Wish I Could Shimmy Like My Sister Kate," to my surprise and delight I heard the recording of my scream.[46]

The Moon Cusser Café opened on the first day of summer in 1963. It was housed in a former grocery, now Basics, the clothing store on Circuit Avenue in Oak Bluffs. In the early 1960s, before the Beatles, before rock went electric, the Moon Cusser was a folkies' hangout, a coffee shop that offered top-of-the-line musicians and a chance for talented amateurs to take the stage.[47]

For baby boomers coming of age on Martha's Vineyard, the Moon Cusser was special. Relatively inexpensive (the cover was $1.50), the café offered musical acts up close. Seating capacity was 125. No alcohol was served. No age restrictions were imposed.[48]

David Lyman, manager of the Moon Cusser, was impressed by the turnout on opening night, featuring the Charles River Valley Boys, a bluegrass band instrumental in rekindling the '60s folk scene. (In 1966, they released *Beatle Country*, a compilation of Beatles tunes in a country style.) The club was packed when the Clancy Brothers[49] arrived. "[The] Clancy boys pushed me aside and took over," recalled Lyman. "They sang rousing Irish drinking songs, told stories, got people singing along. It was a whale of an evening." Throughout the summer of 1963 and for the next two years, Lyman says, "Music became the reason, the driving force behind the Moon Cusser's existence."

A list of those who played at the Moon Cusser reads like a who's who of the '60s: Alan Arkin, Jessie Benton, Jose Feliciano, Mississippi John Hurt, Ian and Sylvia, Bill Keith, Jim Kweskin's Jug Band, Lefty's Bench, Don McLean, Geoff Muldaur, Phil Ochs, Tom Rush and Doc Watson. Manager Lyman recalled: "That spring of 1963, something special happened on the Vineyard, which had an impact on today's music and many of today's musicians."

Moon Cusser memories are poignant. "There was nothing like it on the Vineyard when it opened," the *Gazette* reported, and "when the sun went down, music at the coffee house was a main attraction." Young people appreciated the uniqueness afforded by the Moon Cusser. The first year of the Moon Cusser "seems to be universally burned into the memories of those who were there. It was glorious time for folk music."[50]

Carly Simon turned eighteen the summer the Moon Cusser opened. She said, "It made me inspired to do so much. It obviously had a profound effect on me because I somehow saw it in my mind that I would be singing with a man and that it would be very Vineyard based. And so I felt it very much when I met James Taylor."

The Islanders, a local group made up of Pam Goff, Tom West and Dave Gude,[51] played the Moon Cusser. They sang, played guitar and had a good time. Another group, the Bodes (short for bodacious), included Jack Mayhew, Rick Convery, Charlie Leighton and Jimmy White. The Bodes had a following in the late '60s and still play together decades later.

Tom Rush remembers:[52]

I can tell you that my relationship with the Vineyard started with family visits to my aunt and uncle's "camp" on Chappy [Chappaquiddick]

53

Carly Simon recalled her Moon Cusser days for the *Vineyard Gazette*: "It was thrilling. It was absolutely thrilling. It was the biggest thing that had ever happened to me." *Courtesy of Mark Lovewell.*

when I was 6 or 7, and continued with summers spent at my Aunt Sarah's home in Chilmark in my late teens. I was playing guitar by then, and fell in with a motley assortment of characters that included Davey Gude, Bill Keith, Peter Cohon (now Peter Coyote, the actor), singing "Michael Row the Boat Ashore" at beach parties and such things. The Singing Simon Sisters were just coming on the scene. JT hadn't quite made his presence known.

I indeed came back later, once I'd given up my amateur standing, and played at the Moon Cusser, did concerts at the Tabernacle, the Hot Tin Roof, High School Auditorium, and (my favorite) the Whaling Church. There may well have been others, but they are lost in the mists of time. (The fact that I have so few memories should give an indication of how much fun was being had.)

I do recall that the Moon Cusser had a guest house for visiting artists. And one might well overlap for a few days with musicians coming in ahead of their engagement. I remember getting some hang time with Mississippi John Hurt one year, Ian and Sylvia (Oh, Sylvia!) the next. (Any guy with half a brain was deeply smitten with Sylvia, and none of us could figure out what she saw in this Ian guy, except perhaps that he was tall, handsome, talented, rich, funny and her husband.) The only other thing I can say is that I'm looking forward to my next visit to the Island, whenever that may be.

Dave Lyman reveled as manager of the Moon Cusser: "This was a seven-day-a-week job, but the work was not really work. We loved what we were doing." "Hootenanny" nights were Mondays, when local talent took the stage with an open mic. James Taylor got his start here, and Carly Simon sang with her sister Lucy. As Lyman posted on his website: "I can still see the two Simon sisters, standing there in the spot light, each in a matching delicate white dress, with a guitar, singing 'Winking, Blinking and Nod'…"

Kate Taylor recalls:[53]

When I was a young teenager we could hitch hike all over the island, day and night, and there was no fear. We'd catch a ride down to Circuit Avenue to the Moon Cusser. This was mecca for us. There were many wonderful blues, folk and bluegrass acts on the touring circuit in those days. We could see Josh White, Jr., Doc Watson, the Simon Sisters, Jim Kweskin and the Jug Band, John Hammond, Eric Anderson, Phil Ochs. This was one rich scene.

*I remember watching Maria Muldaur sing those Jug Band songs,
eyes closed, on tiptoe, into the mic. "I'm a Woman." Man, that made
an impression on me. Brother James and his friend Danny "Kootch"
Kortchmar, summer friends who both learned to play guitar, did some of
their first performances there (after some time on stage at the Chilmark
Community Center and around the bonfires at beach parties), and the
crowds loved them. This was the beginning of what has become, for
both of them, lifelong careers in music.*

Kate Taylor speaks for many baby boomers when she says, "We knew
we had it good, but we had no way of knowing just how precious and
golden that era really was."

In 1964, Don Maclean, of "American Pie" fame, assumed the role of
artist in residence at the Moon Cusser. Dave Seward was drawn to the
atmosphere: "I went with my girlfriend, who became my wife, and it seems
we went every night. It was a happening place, and I was in my element."

Seward recalls: "I was a junior in high school, 1963, and Hub Nitchie
was my American history teacher. He loved to make the class come alive.
He would bring in a record player with a Bob Dylan record." Nitchie
believed the banjo was part of American history and encouraged his
students to explore folk music, going so far as to play banjo tunes in his
classroom. Hub Nitchie founded the *Banjo Newsletter* in 1974, now edited
by his son, Donald.

Nitchie and the Seward twins, Dave and Doug, lived in Chilmark in
those halcyon days. Making music accessible promoted folk music on
the Island. "Hub had a tremendous interest in folk music," recalls Dave
Seward. "We became quite good friends. We were into folk music, and
Hub incorporated it into class. We would go over and listen to records
with Hub. He was so enthusiastic about what he was doing." Hub Nitchie
was a memorable man.

Seward was in Hub's class when word of the assassination of President
Kennedy came over the intercom. Rather than talking directly about
the event, Hub listed the presidents who had been assassinated, with
JFK at the end of the list. "It was very moving," says Seward. "He was
still teaching."

One contest left Dave Seward on the sidelines: "That summer of 1964,
we formed a jug band, at Hub Nitchie's suggestion, and entered a contest
at the Unicorn, a coffeehouse in Oak Bluffs similar to the Moon Cusser.
The Unicorn was associated with the Boston coffeehouse of the same

name. Our band was me on kazoo, Doug on jug, John Combra on guitar and Mark Hurd. We played Woody Guthrie's 'This Land Is Your Land' and did very well. We thought we'd won the prize, which was a week's gig at the Boston Unicorn." At the end of the contest, a couple kids took the stage and ran away with their song, winning the contest and heading off to Boston and beyond. The duo was Danny Kortchmar and James Taylor. "We still had a great time," Seward recalls.

Musicians played the Chilmark Community Center in the 1960s, just as Bette and Curley Carroll called square dances in the 1950s. According to the *Vineyard Gazette*, "Musicians took their places on the stage and tuned up for dancing. Suddenly it was Chilmark a Go Go." The Chilmark Community Center was the meeting place for folk musicians to gather. Musicians such as Gale Huntington and Hollis Smith plied their fiddles, Elmer Silva was on guitar and Leonard Athearn and Ernest Correllus strummed their banjos, while Mike Athearn was on the accordion. People came from across the Island.[54]

Gale Huntington's brother Willie had two sons, Peter and Simon, who grew up in a musical environment, playing guitar and singing. Peter Huntington opened for a number of acts, from Bill Stains to John Pousette Dark to Livingston Taylor. Peter's children continue the musical tradition. "Shaelah started violin in first grade and played through college in the orchestra. And she played the flute," says her mother proudly. And, "Aidan started violin at age four, saxophone in third grade and electric bass in seventh grade. He loves jazz." The children grew up in the company of friends and family who encourage music, furthering the tradition of their grandfather and great-uncle.

Like the interconnecting roots of a quaking aspen, musicians relate to one another, learning from their predecessors and following their forebears in style and form, yet stretching, reaching and playing off the shoots and spurs of one another, thus expanding their musical environment.

Chapter 6

THE TAYLOR AGE

Just as the Singing Tiltons gained prominence for their musical prowess in the late nineteenth century, the Taylor siblings earned an impressive reputation for their lyrical accomplishments in the twentieth century. The Taylor family is synonymous with Martha's Vineyard. Five Taylor children were born in successive years, from 1947 to 1951, and spent their formative years summering on Martha's Vineyard.

Alex (1947–1993), the eldest, was a folk and rock musician who recorded two albums, *Dancing with the Devil* and *With Family and Friends,* in the early 1970s. His band was Lucky Strikes, and his voice lent itself to the blues. His songs followed the southern rock vein. Alex often opened for the Allman Brothers Band. His granddaughter Claudia was a high school Minnesinger. His other grandchildren are Caroline, Anna Kate and Paige.

James, the second sibling, was born in 1948.

Kate, or "Sister Kate," formed a band at fifteen and signed a recording contract at nineteen. She recorded *Sister Kate* in 1971, a series of covers and songs written by her brothers. In 1978, she released *Kate Taylor,* which included a duet with James. Her third album, produced by her husband, Charlie Witham, was entitled *Beautiful Road. Kate Taylor Live at the Cutting Room* (2005) includes daughters Aquinnah and Elizabeth, niece Sally Taylor and Carly Simon. *Fair Time* was released in 2009. A *Boston Globe* review called it a "sassy blend of rock and folk and country and soul." The album's songs reflect Kate Taylor's affection for Martha's Vineyard, promoting the solace and charm of the Island.

James Taylor and brother Alex, aboard the *Schamonchi*, fundraising for the Fireman's Association, circa 1988. James's famous song "Sweet Baby James" refers to Alex's son. *Courtesy of Peter Simon.*

Kate is also an accomplished artisan, working with wampum, small beads made of quahog shells, which she uses in jewelry.

Since 1989, Livingston Taylor has been a professor at Boston's Berklee College of Music. Over the course of a year, he performs dozens of concerts. Livingston has an easy-going stage presence, sharing stories and recollections with his audience, making each one a comfortable event.

Livingston Taylor released his album *There You Are Again* in 2006. The *New York Times* characterized it as "a lovely collection, mournful and celebratory, and he credits its existence to the support of an unlikely mentor: his ex-sister-in-law Carly Simon." The article continues: "Livingston Taylor knew Simon for years before she met James; as teenagers and summer pals on Martha's Vineyard." Their friendship dates back more than fifty years, when they performed together at the local movie theater. "The deep connection has endured."[55]

Hugh Taylor, the youngest, has operated the Outermost Inn in Aquinnah since 1989. According to a 2003 interview in the *Boston Globe*, reporter Mary Grauerholz wrote that Hugh "has the handsome Taylor look, sharp blue eyes, rangy build and all. His eyes crinkle when

Stage Performance, by Livingston Taylor, was a book drawn from classroom experiences, coffeehouse gigs and touring with the likes of Jimmy Buffett, Linda Ronstadt and Jethro Tull. *Courtesy of Dan Waters.*

he smiles."[56] He was quoted as saying, "We used to be quite delighted hearing our voices together," says Hugh. "That's what's good about families who sing: They're all pretty tight (sounding)." The newspaper article continues: "Hugh himself has a beautiful voice. He sang for several years at David's Island House in Oak Bluffs, provided backup on his siblings' recordings, and made a demo. He just didn't make the big time." He was invited to sing at David Crohan's birthday celebration at the Tabernacle in 2014.

Rolling Stone portrayed James Taylor as "the archetypal sensitive singer/ songwriter of the Seventies. His songs, especially his early material, were tales of inner torment delivered in low-key tunes, with Taylor's understated tenor backed by intricate acoustic guitar parts that drew on folk and jazz."

The appeal, according to *Rolling Stone*, was that Taylor's songs defined him as "relaxed, personable, and open; his best songs were as artful as they were emotional." His music is his own; his songs, while not folk songs, "were pop compositions with folk dynamics, and in them Taylor put across more bitterness and resignation than reassurance." Conflict and struggle resonate in his music, yet it is artful and reflective of a self-examined life.

And James Taylor, while he may have surmounted the pinnacle of musical success, has not had an easy time. His struggles with addiction are legion. His marriages are multiple. His reclusiveness is acknowledged. Yet even with these issues, he is respected by fellow baby boomers for having endured and survived these life experiences.

When James was twelve, brother Alex convinced him to replace his cello with a guitar. When James and Danny Kortchmar won the Oak Bluffs music contest in 1964, it propelled them on a musical trajectory. Fame was around the corner, yet heroin proved a speed bump along the way. At eighteen, Taylor admitted himself to McLean Psychiatric Hospital in Belmont, just outside Boston. A year later, he took up again with Danny Kortchmar, formed the Flying Machine and made the rounds of Greenwich Village coffeehouses.

The Flying Machine folded in 1968, and Taylor moved to London. He offered a recording of his songs to the A&R man (artists and repertoire talent scout) at the Beatles' newly created Apple Records. Peter Asher, brother of Jane Asher, Paul McCartney's longtime girlfriend and formerly of Peter and Gordon, urged McCartney to sign James Taylor for Apple Records, which proved one of Apple Corps.' few successes. McCartney and George Harrison stopped by the studio as James recorded his eponymous album, which impressed critics but sold poorly.

Taylor returned to the States, spent another stint in a psychiatric hospital and then played in the Newport Folk Festival in 1969. Peter Asher continued as his producer and manager, with the successful release of *Sweet Baby James*, supplemented by Carole King and Danny

Kortchmar. "Fire and Rain," his personal, soul-searching melody, lingered on the pop charts, cresting at number three. That was enough to make the cover of *Time* in 1971 and star in a film, *Two-Lane Blacktop*, with Beach Boy Dennis Wilson.

Mud Slide Slim and the Blue Horizon, his third album, was highlighted by his outstanding rendition of Carole King's "You've Got a Friend." The album sold very well and provided the basis for King and Taylor's continuing professional relationship.

James Taylor and Carly Simon were married in 1972 and divorced in 1983; Carly remains on the Island, as do the Taylor siblings, Livingston, Kate and Hugh, and mother Trudy.

In 2001, and again in 2003, James Taylor won Grammy awards. *Rolling Stone* concluded its piece with admiration for Taylor's lifelong efforts as "one of the most successful touring solo acts of the past forty years."

James Taylor was big in the 1970s, but he was hardly the only show in town. The Skyland Band was prominent, too. Skyland played at the old Seaview, the Boston House and the art workers guild.

Judy Wyle shares her memories:[57] "When I came back East, to live on Martha's Vineyard, I formed the Skyland Band, performing original music with my brother, Rich Johnson, Charlie Leighton, Rick Convery and Jean-Paul Pelletier. That was a fabulous time of my life. It was like a big 'Love-In' when we played."

Memories of musical experiences linger. Betsy Gately recalls Spoof, the first band she played with, in the early 1970s. David Wilson played lead guitar, Merrily Fenner was on bass, Troy Tyson on sax and Nathan Sitkberg on drums. "My favorite musical experience—I still have an inner rock yearning," Betsy Gately recalls wistfully. The group played frequently at Anthony's (now Lola's). "We had a good audience response, playing covers of classic rock, Beatles, Supremes and whatever was on the radio at the time."

Except for during the World Wars, the Vineyard Haven Band always marched in the Memorial Day parade. "Before the war," flutist Martha Child notes, "band members had to pay dues. After the war, it was

Vineyard Haven Band, circa 1954. Martha Child's grandmother Vivian Southwick Mosher played cornet in the 1920s; her father, Gary Mosher, played trumpet for six decades. *Photo by Philip Mosher, courtesy of Martha Child.*

more of a pickup band, a feeling that everyone was able to play." Today, members receive a small stipend.

By the end of the 1940s, the band had shrunk to fewer than twenty members. More musicians were needed. In fact, over the years, the fluctuation of instruments has varied widely. The band played in the new Vineyard Haven bandstand in Owen Park in 1962. An editorial in 1967 worried about "taking the Band for granted."

"In the late 1960s, membership started to dwindle," Martha Child recalls, "and the powers that be decided to let women play." Martha was in the second wave of women. She had always wanted to be in the Vineyard Haven Band but played violin and performed in the Sinfonietta. Her music teacher taught her the flute; at the tender age of twelve, Martha joined the band.

She said, "Sometimes I think my favorite part of the playing season is the beginning and the end, but seriously, I take pride that I've lasted this long."

In a letter to the *Gazette* in 1971, band historian Tom Bardwell proudly noted that the band performed background music for Katharine Cornell's movie *This Is Our Island*, her celebration of Tisbury's tercentennial.

Bardwell worried that the band would fold from disinterest, but a savior was found. "Bob Nute kindly and wonderfully took over; the two of us saved the Vineyard Haven Band from extinction," said Bardwell. Nute was the high school music teacher. "He was a trained music educator."

Only thirteen musicians showed up to his first rehearsal. The biggest frustration was when key musicians failed to show, as when not a single trombone player was present for Meredith Wilson's "76 Trombones." Bob Nute enticed his students to join the band. "This caused a problem with flute students to let them all play," Bardwell observed, dryly. "Upper voice of band was a flute-oriented flute presentation. All you could hear was flutes. Screeching havoc of flutes! That stringy upper sound was very objectionable." Bardwell feared the cornets and trumpets "were all drowned out," but the band got through it.

The (1977) *Tisbury Town Report* was dedicated to the Vineyard Haven Band. Tom Bardwell wrote, "And several years ago it [the band] was called upon to play a special 'Stand Up' concert for Senator Edward W. Brooke as a salute and tribute to his Island ties and connections." The piece continued, "The band has become a symbol of the universality of music, and many of its member families have supported it and played in it for generations."

By the time he retired in 1981, Bob Nute had built the band to nearly ninety musicians, so crowded on the Oak Bluffs bandstand that members took turns playing. He said, "They all show up for Illumination Night. That's when they produce. People make the effort to get it together for that one night." He added, "It's an old Island tradition that goes way back, a real old New England event."

Chapter 7

FANTASY ISLAND

"I had gone to pick up a friend at the Boston House on Circuit Avenue in Oak Bluffs." Bonnie McElaney Menton has a clear recollection of an evening forty years ago. "My friend Jackie said, 'John Lennon is here.' We ran over to his car, parked right there on Circuit Avenue. It was a Maserati with the door that rose up. We poked our heads in the passenger-side window, where he was sitting. 'I can't believe you're here,' Jackie said. 'We'll give you a tour of the Island.'"

It was September 15, 1975, just weeks before John Lennon's son Sean was born. Bonnie continues: "We were in the process of moving from a cabin in the woods to a big old sea captain's house in Vineyard Haven. We parked his Maserati there, as it was so conspicuous. And we took him on a tour in my friend Jackie's big Buick Skylark. We stopped at the cabin in West Tisbury, where our three-legged Irish setter came out to greet us. There was a hatchet on a stump. John Lennon looked at the hatchet and the three-legged dog and said, 'What are you, the Manson girls?'"

Lennon offered to take the girls to dinner at Shiretown in Edgartown. The girls were waitresses at the Colonial Inn or Harborside, and "word spread quickly through the working community: 'We're going to dinner with John Lennon.'"

"I remember it was Yom Kippur because Judy said, 'I can't eat, I'm fasting,' and I said, 'You have to order something. John Lennon is taking us to dinner.'" She explains, "We were all trying to be cool. We tried to seem like it was not a big deal, but we were like in shock. It was hard to know how to act. We were shy, but he put us at ease and it was comfortable, but there were moments of unease."

One girl said Lennon looked just like his photographs. He replied, "Don't you?"

The girls drove to Menemsha to see the sunset. Lennon said Martha's Vineyard reminded him of Scotland. Back at the sea captain's house, the girls offered Lennon a bedroom with a sleigh bed, with a chenille bedspread, and he went to bed.

"Jackie couldn't believe he was really here, so she knocked on his door, opened it and said, 'I just came to wish you good night.' Lennon, wrapped in his bedspread, came out and said to us, 'Someone just woke me up to say goodnight.'" Bonnie continues: "We three girls, Jackie, Judy and me, sat up talking with John Lennon until it must have been two in the morning. He said it reminded him of a Scottish girls school." Eventually, everyone went off to bed.

The memory lingers. "I can still picture him at the Shiretown Inn having dinner or coming downstairs in the morning, wrapped in a chenille bedspread." She feels it is "so good to re-tell the story, as it happened back in the '70s, and we didn't talk about it for a long time." She smiles, "It really happened."

Other Islanders have memorable stories of meeting famous musicians—or near misses. In the mid-1970s, my wife was pregnant—very pregnant. It was only a few days before her due date when a story circulated that Elvis Presley was on the Vineyard. Squeezing into a friend's VW bug, the two women drove from one end of Martha's Vineyard to the other, searching for the elusive King. Everywhere they went, they heard he was just down the road, ahead of them, in the next town. They never caught up with Elvis, but the story lingers.

Diana Ross of the Supremes vacationed on the Vineyard. She rented a house in Chilmark. (I had the honor of dancing with Diana Ross in 1997. I use the term loosely. We both had daughters graduating from Georgetown University. At an event, Diana Ross and I were on the dance floor at the same time, though not together. I did nod in her direction.)

Keith Richards has visited the Vineyard, dining at Atria in Edgartown and jumping on stage at the Hot Tin Roof. He plucked a few chords, but

Carly Simon sang on the shores of Menemsha in her 1987 HBO concert, with family and friends. *Courtesy of Peter Simon.*

it was not a concert. Paul McCartney attended a wedding on the Island and caught the eye of a guest. He played his guitar in a jam session. Lionel Ritchie vacationed at Shearer Cottage in Oak Bluffs, played at local clubs with the Commodores and sang at a Shearer family wedding.

Another prominent musician, Carly Simon, lives on the Vineyard. I spoke with her in a parking lot. At the time, I was administrator of the local nursing home, and Carly offered to sing to the residents. I wanted to attend but chose not to. Staff members stood in the doorway of the dining room and were treated to a holiday concert. When I ran into Carly in the parking lot, I asked how it went. She said the staff members enjoyed the music, but she felt the residents hardly knew she was there. One resident fell asleep, her head nodding dangerously near her mashed potatoes. Maybe they just weren't ready for her.

And of course, the name Bruce Springsteen sparks a story—or should we say, an "almost story." The daughter of a Vineyard couple dated Springsteen's son in college. At graduation, Bruce invited the girl and her parents out to dinner. Bruce and the girl's father—let's call him Al— discussed Al's need to reinvent himself in a new career. Bruce said he had to reinvent himself each time he recorded a new album. The men bonded. And the wife—let's call her Sue—invited the Springsteens to the

Bill and Hillary Clinton joined the Flying Elbows on stage. Walter Cronkite sat in with the band once as well. *Courtesy of Nancy Jephcote.*

Vineyard. Unfortunately, Bruce's son and the girl broke up, so Bruce lost his Vineyard invite.

President Clinton, during his annual vacation, was the subject of many musical experiences. I was a limo driver for Bill Clinton's sixtieth birthday celebration. While waiting for the party to break up, I wandered over to the food table, by the party tent. A caterer said, "We just cut the birthday cake, take a slice." I did. And I took a big bite.

From behind the tent flap came Bill Clinton, saxophone slung over his shoulder. "What shall I play?" the president asked me. I tried to chew, swallow and answer all at once, and it came out garbled, confused and disjointed. "Play Happy Birthday, Mr. President," I tried to say.

Well, he did. But it was full of squeaks and squawks. I felt awkward. Clinton looked pleased. The tent flap pushed aside again, and a musician called the president back to the party.

I was so relieved!

And if there's one Bill Clinton story, there's sure to be another. A tale from saxophonist Steve Tully:

> *I was playing for a fundraiser in Edgartown, in the last year of Clinton's presidency, and Hillary was getting ready to run for the Senate in New York. I was there with Jeremy Berlin on keyboards and his brother Matt on bass. They were about to introduce Hillary Clinton to the crowd.*

Well, I'm watching her, and I felt this hand on my shoulder, and President Clinton leaned in and said, "That's a fine-looking saxophone you have there." He started to tell me about a saxophone he had, and his voice was loud, and people were listening to him rather than the person introducing Hillary.

Someone snapped a photograph of the president and me, and Matt and Jeremy, just at the moment Hillary said, "Shhhhh, Bill." Our faces are filled with surprise as we were caught in the moment.

And then there's a tale of a Vineyard name from yesteryear. Bob Hammond, of the Flying Elbows, recalled Gale Huntington, the fiddler: "He [Huntington] played earlier with a number of fiddlers and told tales of how ships had fiddlers aboard ship to keep the sailors happy. There was such energy in these folksingers through the years they sang together."

Chapter 8

YOU WIN SOME, YOU LOSE SOME

Bob Hammond was an original member of the Flying Elbows, a fiddle group that he says represents only a tiny microcosm of the Vineyard music scene. Hammond recalls the early days, when fiddlers played with the group, left for another opportunity, returned and then moved on again. "All these branches get tangled up and crossed over; it's like walking through the Vineyard woods," he says. The Flying Elbows have adapted to the changing scene over the years, and today, forty years out, they're better than ever.

The genesis of the Flying Elbows, in 1976, was the gathering of a few friends who played in different fiddle groups. "What pulled it together," recalls Bob Hammond, "was meeting for jam sessions in the Topside room at the Ritz. Spencer Welch was a gifted piano player, who was very much at the center, playing stride and boogie styles surrounded by various stringed instruments. Most of us were college students, both summer and local kids, in our early twenties. It was casual and a lot of fun."

"Someone threw out the name Johnny Quitsa and the Flying Elbows [for the group], and Flying Elbows stuck. For me, that's where it began," says Hammond. "I'm the only one who can go back that far."

At a gig at the Oceanview, the Elbows met Denny Alexander, who was in charge of the Agricultural Fair at the Grange Hall for 1977. A fiddle contest was broached. Bob Hammond agreed to run it but gave no thought to rules or judges or prizes. He said, "I looked to get a bunch of musicians together to have fun."[58] Judges were designated, a sound

"We were made up of people of varying ability, just coming together to play," recalls Bob Hammond. "The Flying Elbows has become well defined over the years." Pictured are Bob Hammond and Nancy Jephcote. *Courtesy of Dan Waters.*

Opposite: The Flying Elbows, of which Tom Hodgson (pictured) is a member, began as a loose collaboration of fiddlers but coalesced for summer gigs. "Sometimes we'd even have two gigs at once," recalls Bob Hammond. "That happened in this community of music on the Vineyard." *Courtesy of Dan Waters.*

system was located and promotion happened via the pre-Facebook social network. "It got big fast! An amazing number of talented fiddlers came out of the woodwork. The contest was so successful it shut down the fair—literally—for about forty-five minutes. We blew out the main electrical circuits!"[59]

One memorable party involved Lady Bird Johnson, who, according to Bob Hammond, wanted "a bluegrass band for her July 4th party. We were the group closest to bluegrass; I guess it was the

fiddle, which qualified us. Lady Bird dictated what kind of music to play. We even had to play 'Mack the Knife.' That's the time Walter Cronkite was up on stage with us."

Monthly contradances at the Chilmark Community Center led to the group's longevity. The Flying Elbows played at Wintertide, as it migrated from the Stone Church to Five Corners. Musing on his memories, Bob Hammond says, "I feel lucky to have touched part of this, to play with other great musicians, especially in the early years." He adds, "The Flying

The Flying Elbows are a fixture at the annual Tisbury picnic and play numerous fundraisers across the Island. *Clockwise from center*: Nancy Jephcote, Paul Thurlow, Bob Hammond, Brian Weiland and Tom Hodgson. *Courtesy of Ray Ewing for the* Vineyard Gazette, *used with permission.*

Elbows strove to keep closer to traditional fiddle music. A lot of people came and left, cycled through the group, sometimes to play for a musical weekend, sometimes for the summer. It was a loose collaboration."

They have been "an important part of the general music of the community," says Hammond, who left the group himself for a few years.

Hammond says, "The current incarnation has been playing together for a while. Paul Thurlow plays funk and jazz piano; Brian Weiland is a musical chameleon. Everyone's always going in different directions, it's whoever can show up." Tom Hodgson enjoys his role in the band. Nancy Jephcote is the de facto leader. "All of us play in different bands," Hammond explains.

"Live music here has never been confined by walls," wrote Linda Black in her comprehensive music review in 2009. "Pretty much every area of the Island has a history of outdoor concerts."[60]

A case in point was the No Nukes Concert held on the rolling hills of Chilmark's Allen Farm above the seaside allure of Lucy Vincent Beach. The *Vineyard Gazette* reported, "The No Nukes Festival in 1978 drew some 6,500 people to the Allen Farm, where Carly Simon, Kate and Alex Taylor and John Hall performed…Surely never had Chilmark seen anything like it." Peter Simon, who helped coordinate it, was quoted as saying that music "was the galvanizing force that influenced our thinking."[61] The Chilmark fest proved a prototype for the No-Nuke Concert at Madison Square Garden the following year.

Linda Black described the Chilmark event: "The gods were smiling down, with one of those quintessential fall days—a blue sky dotted with a few milky clouds and a warm breeze rippling the sparkling waters of the Atlantic and the expanse of green fields housing a veritable sea of onlookers. And the Island muses were in full force too, with Carly and James, along with John Hall of Hall and Oates, performing on a makeshift stage. Cast against that farm background, it was decidedly reminiscent of the iconic Woodstock festival."[62]

Carly Simon has been an Island presence for half a century. She was interviewed by Matthew Perzanowski for West Tisbury's *School's Out* in 2013. She told him she became a singer because, as a child, she stuttered. "She thought singing was easier than talking, so she became a singer and songwriter," wrote Perzanowski. She always loved to sing but suffered from stage fright.

Top: Sally Taylor, daughter of Carly Simon and James Taylor, keeps the family legend alive. *Courtesy of Dan Waters.*

Left: Ben Taylor pursues the family musical tradition. *Courtesy of Dan Waters.*

Among her influences, she cites Odetta, Peggy Lee and Judy Collins. Describing her greatest accomplishment, she said, "When I won the Academy Award for a song called 'Let the River Run,' it was a huge achievement." Of course, she was asked about "You're So Vain." "To her, it is not that interesting because she was there and she wrote it, so it's not really a mystery to her," noted Perzanowski.

George Brush and Herb Putnam came up with the concept of a full-service nightclub for Martha's Vineyard. They broached the idea to Carly Simon at the No Nukes Concert, and by the spring of 1979, she was on board, and the Hot Tin Roof was on its way.

The name was suggested by James Taylor, and it is of interest that folksinger Burl Ives gained fame for his movie role in *Cat on a Hot Tin Roof*. Coincidence?

The Hot Tin Roof was situated on grounds by the Martha's Vineyard Airport, a "roadhouse out in the middle of the woods, where the only neighbors were skunks, raccoons, and ticks." It held three hundred people, "where rank-and-file Islanders could share the dance floor with an astonishing number of head-turning celebrities, from John Belushi to John Travolta and Jackie Onassis."[63] While Margot Datz was painting the iconic murals along the walls, John Belushi strolled in and twirled her across the dance floor.

The club opened on June 7, 1979. "The celebrity element helped launch the Hot Tin Roof," Burrell wrote. "It embodied something cool and hip, but it was also laid back, embracing the mix of the Island. An aura grew around the Hot Tin Roof." With Belushi and Dan Ackroyd's brother, the Hot Tin Roof proved a mecca for celebrities and those who sought to be seen with them.

Prior to music videos, bands would have to play the concert circuit to promote their music. Big-name performers at the Hot Tin Roof included Peter Tosh, Cyndi Lauper, Ricky Nelson, Martin Mull and Steven Wright, among many others.

One night, manager Tim Mathiesen glanced over the stage and out to the nearby trees and realized fans were clinging to the branches, trying to get a glimpse of Peter Tosh on stage. As local legend Bob Lee recalled, "Word spread fast. The place got a great rep." Lee was tour director for Kate Taylor's band, Skin Tight.

Tom Rush recalled that his gig at the Roof "was disrupted a bit when JT came in with John Belushi, who was in a rowdy mood, or in touch with a higher reality of some sort. James did his best to quiet him down,

Tom Rush, seen here in 1982, has performed at the Moon Cusser, the Hot Tin Roof and the Whaling Church. He loves to play on the Vineyard. *Courtesy of Alison Shaw.*

but the noise from the bar was such that I cut my set short." Stories circulate decades later.

In the early 1980s, Jimmy Burgoff's Tisbury Jazz All-Stars—Jeremy Berlin, Lenny Yancey, Ed Larkosh and Jimmy B.—opened at the Hot Tin Roof for acts such as Dizzy Gillespie, Joe Williams, Dave Brubeck and Ramsey Lewis. "We were treated with respect by the management and fellow musicians," says Jimmy B. "One time I was walking my bass back to the dressing room, and Dizzy himself stopped me, lightly patted my butt and said, 'You play good, boy!' Then he let loose with a puff of cigar smoke that caused me to cough right in his face."

Kate Taylor shares a poignant recollection:

> *There were some memorable nights at the Hot Tin Roof in the early days of that place. It was smoking in there. One of these nights, we had all of us on stage with a seven-piece band, horns, keyboards, guitars, drums, bass guitars. We were stoked. There wasn't room to fit a paper*

Kate Taylor said of the Hot Tin Roof: "There were several nights when all of my brothers and I performed there together." *Courtesy of Dan Waters.*

clip on stage. All of a sudden who should appear in the wings but John Belushi! With his uncanny physical agility and grace, he did a couple of cartwheels across the front of the stage, grabbed a mic, sang a couple of numbers and waved good-bye to the screaming crowd. He proclaimed, "I be leaving this island" and headed off to a waiting airplane. He flew off to Los Angeles for some meetings. We were never to see him again.[64]

Fans appreciated the varied musical styles. The Roof drew "a cross-section of talent: reggae, blues, jazz and the old Motown acts," according to Bob Lee. Willie Dixon, Jimmy Cliff and Dizzy Gillespie performed. Walter Cronkite, Bill Styron and Bill Murray were there, taking in the scene.

Yet it didn't last. By the mid-1980s, the Hot Tin Roof drifted into obscurity, was sold in 1986 to Peter Martell and then fell into bankruptcy.

In a very different venue with a very different program, a historical musical concert was performed at the Old Whaling Church in 1982, entitled "Three Hundred Years of Music on Martha's Vineyard." The intent was to perform memorable musical pieces, ranging from the Bay Psalm Book of 1698, to the Apollo Harmony collection of 1807, to nineteenth-century whaling chanteys through early twentieth-century compositions by bandleader Will Hardy.

The concert playlist exemplified American music in a classless society, offering music to rich and poor alike. Music was an integral element of the American experience, not just the dominion of the elite but appreciated by all economic and social classes.

The concert celebrated the fiddle playing of Gale Huntington, "who is something of a folk hero to Island musicologists and beyond."[65] Instruments from early eras and period clothing added to the atmosphere.

"The chorus performed Will Hardy's 'Tivoli Girl,' a song made popular at Mr. Hardy's public dance hall (the Tivoli) in Oak Bluffs during the roaring '20s," the *Gazette* reported proudly.

Bringing folk music into the current era, the *Gazette* noted, "Thomas Hart Benton was a virtuoso harmonica player and lover of folk music and folk-inspired music." The article added: "Two unusual and unjustly neglected suites for harmonica, flute and harpsichord, 'Chilmark Suite' and 'Gay Head Dances,' were composed for and dedicated to Tom and Rita Benton by frequent Vineyard resident, Edward Robinson."[66]

The rebirth of the Hot Tin Roof occurred in 1995, when Carly Simon revived, renovated and rejuvenated the structure, expanding seating capacity to eight hundred. "Within a short time, the Hot Tin Roof was again a celebrity hang-out for the likes of President Bill Clinton, Prince Andrew, Diane Sawyer and Keith Richards."[67] Chris Burrell, in his article for *Martha's Vineyard Magazine*, added, "In its heyday, the Hot Tin Roof functioned as ground zero for Vineyard nightlife. In addition to the performers, there were celebrities. But beyond the glitz, there was the music."

The goal had been to revive this landmark by offering a variety of music. Herb Putnam, one of the founders, was quoted as saying, "We resurrected a center for music and we were successful in trying to provide a very wide cross section of entertainment, from oldies to the Cuban Latin influence."[68]

It was not enough. Tom Major, a founder of the band Entrain, noted, "With your heavyweight acts, the room was too small, but with too many of the acts, people didn't come out to support them." The only way to make money was to fill the seats; if people didn't come, the seats sat empty.

By 2000, the Hot Tin Roof closed again. Proprietors believed the Vineyard population had aged and was less attracted to a wild nightlife. More stringent liquor license laws were imposed. Penalties for driving under the influence of alcohol were more prevalent and severe.[69]

After the Hot Tin Roof closed in 2001, Outerland occupied the site in 2006, followed by Nectars MV in 2009, followed by Flatbread, which purchased the property in 2012. The 2013 season opened at Flatbread with two popular Vineyard bands, Good Night Louise and Johnny Hoy and the Bluefish.

From the major musical performances of contradances by the Flying Elbows to main acts at the Hot Tin Roof, music reigns supreme on Martha's Vineyard. Not to be overshadowed by the big names, Frank and Peter Dunkl, of the Vineyard Haven Band, have gathered a few musicians together each year to play brass instruments at public events during the holiday season. Ed Rogers, Shawna Nute and others join the Dunkl brothers. As Katie Carroll reported, "The Vineyard Haven Brass Band, with local celebrities the Dunkls, will be sure to delight."[70] Their music is another element in the musical tradition that continues to burnish the Vineyard's reputation.

Chapter 9

NURTURANCE

S tories of the Wintertide are rife with rumor about its founding and funding. Wintertide was designed to offer "a place, from October to May, where the population of eighteen- to twenty-nine-year-olds could gather to listen to and perform music and poetry,"[71] according to Sherm Goldstein, director at Martha's Vineyard Community Services (MVCS) in the 1970s. "It was funded through a drug prevention grant I wrote to the Massachusetts Department of Mental Health. My memory is that I initially applied for a $2,500 grant. After writing it, I realized no one would spend that much time and effort for a couple of thousand bucks and went through the mimeographs and added another zero." Thus, Wintertide began with a healthy state endowment.

Wintertide opened in 1976. Pastor Don Lyons was on the MVCS board. Pastors Leon and Helen Oliver of the Methodist (Stone) Church were involved. Sherm Goldstein recalled: "Wintertide was held every Monday evening and initially housed in the downstairs of the Patisserie on Main Street, Vineyard Haven. Later it moved to the basement of the Stone Church."

Performers included Mark Lovewell, Tristan Israel, Ellen Epstein, Cindy Kallett and Mike Hayden, among many others. Following Community Services' involvement, "Edie and I ran Wintertide for two years at the Wooden Tent," recalls Kathy Rose. "It was glorious.

We started Patty Larkin on her career. Had Craig Kingsbury come to play. That was early or middle '80s." Wintertide then became autonomous and moved to Five Corners.

Wintertide Coffeehouse became the symbol of the unique musical nature that flourished on the Island in the last quarter of the twentieth century. The emphasis was on "winter" to provide a venue in the off-season. Many locals frequented Wintertide, as well as those from the mainland. They came to share their music, garner performing experience and revel in the atmosphere. Open mic nights offered a venue for novices. Nationally recognized artists enjoyed playing there.

Tony Lombardi, Wintertide director from 1988 to 1998, dismisses spirituality or "magicality" as the reason so many of the greats of folk, rock-and-roll, folk rock, pop rock, jazz, blues and country came to play their chords and engage their audience at Wintertide. The growing tide of singer/songwriters appreciated the laid-back environment. Many musicians were part of the scene, from the legendary Odetta and Dave Van Ronk to Ramblin' Jack Elliot and Iris Dement.

Lombardi speculates that the Vineyard's compelling attraction for musicians is tangible, observable and scientific, like the seven world vortexes that function with special qualities supposedly due to a complex of subsurface magnetic fields. (Jerry Muskin muses: "My wife and I experienced the power of vortexes in Glastonbury, England, and Sedona, Arizona.") Perhaps "the surrounding sea," as Mark Lovewell hypothesizes, is an answer. Yet the fact remains that music is central to the Vineyard's culture. It attracts and grows musicians like no other place.

"Creative people seem to be drawn to the Vineyard, especially those who practice the musical arts," says Tony Lombardi. Musicians who remain, do so, it seems, because the energy compels them to stay; it gives them a harbor in which to create, surrounded by a community of kindred souls who encourage their creations being brought to life. Prominent musicians came to Wintertide, as well as fledgling performers new to the craft at the time, such as Martin Sexton, Patty Griffin and Mary Gauthier.

"Other artists from around the world were attracted not by money but by the spirit of this place," says Tony Lombardi. "It is impossible to quantify the impact the Island and places like Wintertide have had on the world stage, but surely it is huge." Five historic albums document the moment in time that was Wintertide.

Rick Bausman (right), of the Drum Workshop, plays with music producer Jim Parr. *Courtesy of Rick Bausman.*

Susanna Sturgis recalls her musical introduction to the Vineyard:

Not long after I moved to the Vineyard year-round, I started volunteering at Wintertide Coffeehouse, generally learning my way around the island's grassroots music scene. Die Kunst der Drum (DKDD), an all-drum [ensemble], was prominent at that time. They played inside, they played on the beach, and wherever they played, people got up and danced.

I couldn't help noticing that DKDD was almost entirely male. Roberta was one of the two exceptions. Co-leader of the ensemble was Rick Bausman, who went on to found the remarkable Drum Workshop. I took a class with Rick at Wintertide in its year-round Five Corners incarnation. Both Roberta and Rick are huge believers in building community through music.[72]

Rick Bausman has a goal to "build a community through ensemble drumming with a therapeutic component." His Drum Workshop plays an integral role in the Vineyard community.

Bausman came to the Vineyard as a volunteer with Camp Jabberwocky, the cerebral palsy summer program, in 1980. He worked with a young man, Rob, with developmental disabilities, so, in Rick's words, "Camp Jabberwocky brought me here, and working with Rob kept me here." He met fellow drummers, and "they got together for fun, to learn traditional ensemble drumming" of West Africa and Cuba and Haiti. Sam Holmstock led the group; later Bausman took over.

Bausman learned drumming skills from masters. John Amira, of New York, taught Haitian drumming, which became Bausman's primary expertise; he now knows more traditional Haitian drumming than that of any other culture. "One thing that's extremely important to me is that I learn, perform and pass on the music accurately. I am a repository of these original rhythms," says Bausman.

Teachers across the Vineyard requested that Rick share his program. He began with younger students and progressed through middle and high-school students. The program took off in the late 1980s. "It was happening," he recalled with pleasure. He formalized the effort, calling it the Drum Workshop; he is the founder, director and sole employee.

By introducing the Drum Workshop to the school system, it became apparent that the program was not only educational but also therapeutic. A teacher "had a group of kids who had a very, very hard time in school." She asked Rick if he thought drumming might help. He said, "Yes." Another person asked Rick if he thought drumming would be appropriate for senior citizens. Yes. He always says yes. And kids on the Asperger's spectrum? Yes again.

Singer/songwriter Michael Johnson had an Island band, Miracle Cure, from 1991 to 1995, during what he calls "the golden age of Island music." He explains, "We played rhythm and blues, funk reggae, gospel. We played all of the clubs and parties and did a gospel brunch at Lola's restaurant [in the] summer of '95." That gospel brunch was "the best gig ever."

Michael Johnson is black. "There was a paucity of black music played by black artists on Island for many cultural/ economic reasons, some obvious some not. [Thus] most of the black music was played by white bands."

Rick Bausman was in Miracle Cure. He remembered, "Michael was a joy to work with. He is a true artist and showman. It was crucial to him that every show was as good as it could be, and he always gave it his very best. He really respected and enjoyed the audience and was contagiously delighted when we were playing well and the music was hot."

Imagine discussing music on the Vineyard over the last forty-five years without mentioning the Taylor family and Carly Simon. Look at Livestock '95, a fundraising event (a Vineyard musical fixture) to cover the costs of the new Agricultural Society barn. From planning through performance, an enormous level of excitement prevailed.

Why? Carly Simon and James Taylor had started their remarkable careers on the Island and achieved the heights having burnished the Vineyard brand here. It was the first time since their (1972–83) marriage that Carly and James would appear together. Their performance garnered unmatched attention for the event.

The late satirist Art Buchwald summered on Martha's Vineyard; his columns were published worldwide. He exposed the deep divide that occurred in the days leading up to the concert:[73]

> *Americans are lethargic about most things. The only one that seems to make them willing to lay down their lives is a big-name concert.*
>
> *That is why historians are still pondering how World War III started on Martha's Vineyard. Their conclusion is that it originated in August 1995.*
>
> *The Agricultural Hall trustees decided to have a concert to raise money for its roof. They persuaded singers Carly Simon and James Taylor to reunite. At the time, it sounded like a good idea. But when word got out, all hell broke loose. It was carried on radio and television and the Internet from Nantucket to New Zealand.*
>
> *When tickets were put on sale, they were gobbled up in a matter of minutes, and suddenly this tight little island was divided between those who held seats and those who didn't. Once again, a conflict was created between the Haves and Have-Nots, which could lead only to terrible things.*

James Taylor and Carly Simon were married in 1972 and had two children: Sarah, known as Sally, and Benjamin. James and Carly reunited for the Livestock '95 concert. *Courtesy of Peter Simon.*

The first hostilities broke out when a man in Menemsha accused a fisherman of stealing his tickets from his pocket at the Home Port Restaurant. The lobsterman said it was a lie. He said he found his tickets in a lobster pot off Gay Head.

Jerry Muskin recalls, "I helped set up the chairs, and I can tell you the excitement, even for the volunteers, was palpable. Tickets sold out immediately. When Carly and James broke into their signature duets, the crowd of ten thousand roared, demonstrating their regard for the one-time couple and their music. If there had already been a roof, it would been have blown off."

Chapter 10

OFF THE BEATEN PATH

William Waterway was introduced to the Native American flute during a cross-country venture, on horseback, in the 1970s. He recalls, "I was camping near the Gila Indian Reservation in Arizona when I heard this eerie, soul-entrancing music filling the night air. Besides my response, there was the response of my two horses, who lifted their heads and pointed their ears in the direction of the music."

Over the years, Waterway learned to play the Native American flute. With like-minded people, he formed a group on-Island, which played for

R. Carlos Nakai (left) and William Waterway at Nakai's Native American flute workshop in Montana. *Courtesy of William Waterway.*

William Waterway playing flute meditation beneath the endangered Gay Head Lighthouse. The History Press published his book *Gay Head Lighthouse* in 2014. *Courtesy of William Waterway.*

Opposite, top: William Waterway celebrating New Year's Eve 2013–14 inside the lighting room atop the Gay Head Lighthouse. *Courtesy of William Waterway.*

Opposite, bottom: William Waterway and singer/songwriter Sharon Benson performing a water song at Central Park Bandshell. *Courtesy of William Waterway.*

several years. In 2007, William spent a couple weeks in Montana with fellow flutists, studying the art of the flute under Carlos Nakai, one of the foremost Native American flutists. "Truly, a transforming experience," Waterway says.

William Waterway has performed in venues across the Island, from Featherstone's summer solstice to Pathways, both solo and with David Stanwood, and at the Yard, where he "played ten different flutes to ten different dance movements." Off-Island, Waterway has performed at art galleries, weddings and memorial services, in New York, at Central Park and the United Nations and with celebrities such as David Carradine and Pete Seeger.

William Waterway is not the only Vineyarder who pursues an atypical musical vision. While Waterway dabbles in the somewhat unusual Native American flute, Jay Segel makes music, literally.

"I was a musician before I was a physician," says the podiatrist, who neatly blends the two careers. Music and podiatry are disciplines at which he both enjoys and excels. Jay Segel is a songwriter whose works date back thirty years. From love songs to lullabies, from folk to rock, he's done it all.

As he muses over his extensive body of work, he sees "the economy of verbiage. When you have three or four minutes to get your point across, you have to choose your words very carefully." He challenges himself to find the right words to express his emotions economically.

He explains his process of composing: "I write most of the songs myself, then run them by my best friend, my writing partner, Mark Cohen, who played a lot at Wintertide. He has great ears, does most of the recording and mixing with me, and we go back and forth in arranging a song in many ways. It helps to give me perspective." Working together, they reach "the kernel of something that's there."

Rick Bausman and Jim Parr are part of the process as well. Dr. Segel explains, "You have to communicate to the players. You have to tell them what's on your mind and where you are. And then you stand back and let great players do great things and they give you more than you could have asked for, things you didn't even know you wanted."

His song "Cozy" is about the process of creating a song. He said, "If I went to sleep with the idea, and had been playing the guitar, and I got a chord pattern I liked, it's almost like the chord pattern and the things I thought about would translate into music and a melody and a couplet." Here are some lines from "Cozy":

> *the rhythm running thru me*
> *the chords are coming quickly*
> *with the lyrics she left me*
> *I know she's talking thru me*

Working with Rick Bausman, Dr. Segel says, "Repetitive motions will help the neurological system. Remembering patterns and then changing patterns keeps your brain working. You remind the body of what it always knew and promote that interaction between body and mind for better function." Dr. Segel is excited about the possibilities of drumming and improved motor coordination, but like Rick Bausman, he is cautious about moving too fast.

Vineyard musicians are not limited by the boundaries of the island. While Waterway plays his flute, and Segel creates his medleys, Rick Bausman travels abroad to spread his message.

Bausman took his Drum Workshop off-Island—way off-Island—all the way to Africa. As a drum instructor, Bausman has prepared curriculum manuals for drumming. "I have a very solid roster, an arsenal of activities that I use to reach different people who have differing abilities," he says, "and that was developed right here, in this laboratory that we call Martha's Vineyard."

He brought the manuals and a dozen drums to a school in Zambia that has a strong drumming tradition. Their attitude, however, was that if you are disabled, you can't play the drum. "I brought the opposite attitude," says Rick, who played with local drummers in the village of Mukuni. "The drummers thought I was 'wicked cool.' That was the translation."

Rick taught class in the school and then invited a young man, Foster Wachata, to work with thirty-five students, ensuring they continue to drum once a week. Local children had grown up in a drumming culture, but no one thought they could drum. Bausman says, "They were excited, energized, inspired by the experience."

At the end of his ten-day adventure, Rick Bausman and the Zambian drummers gathered under a great tree in the village square, and hundreds came to an impromptu concert. Bausman said, "And I was right in the

Rick Bausman teaching a class in Zambia, Africa. "It was an enormous thrill to play with them," he says. *Courtesy of Rick Bausman.*

middle of it. It was an enormous thrill for me, to share with them, and for that moment, I was part of the village life."

He works "all over Martha's Vineyard. I participate in the public schools, in Community Services with the elderly and I work through the Councils on Aging."

The Drum Workshop creates a community through ensemble drumming. Whether participants are children or senior citizens, experienced or novices, the Drum Workshop includes them in the therapeutic angle of drumming, as an enthusiastic, enriching experience.

One young man credits the Vineyard with starting him on a musical career. Hudson Bausman says, "I discovered how amazing it felt to share music with people." He was a counselor at Camp Jabberwocky with his father, Rick. "I gained a level of confidence, but more importantly I learned that teaching is about progress, not competition."

Working with students of varying age and ability, he says, "My only goal was for us to make music together." He adds, "Everyone deserves to be happy and experience the one-of-a-kind stress relief [that] music can provide."

Maddie Scott has been playing drums since she was eleven and playing piano since she was fifteen. Now seventeen, she is headed off to college. The Vineyard became her launching pad. She has performed with the Minnesingers and Vineyard Haven Band and plays open mic at the Y, where she recorded songs in the studio. Her band performed there.

Without the Vineyard, Maddie says, "I don't think I would have been able to go to college for music, or hope to have a career in music. I've made so many connections, and so many people have given me great advice here." She is on the road to a musical career and hopes to become a session drummer or private instructor.

The Martha's Vineyard YMCA, which opened in 2010, created a Wintertide Collective, with a show by acclaimed singer/songwriter Ellis Paul.[74] His performance was held at Alex's Place, the Y's teen center.[75] "Mr. Paul was a fixture at Vineyard Haven's Wintertide Coffeehouse. This year [2012] marks the first return of both Wintertide and Mr. Paul to the Island," wrote Naomi Pallas.[76]

Mr. Paul told the *Times*, "I love the Vineyard. It's a community of artistic people who understand art differently than on the mainland, and I think there's some magic in starting up an artistic place for it." Ms. Pallas's article continues: "The Wintertide Collective has taken the place of The Base, at the Alexandra Gagnon Teen Center at the YMCA. It is a black-box-style performance space for artists of all sorts that also acts as a recording studio, dance hall, and practice space. It will host shows for national and local talents, including up-and-coming teen musicians." The program offers an entertainment venue with the opportunity for teens to learn about promoting performances, the music business and back-stage concert experience.

"The Wintertide Collective idea relates back to the original coffeehouse," says Tony Lombardi. "It is that kids and the community can come together in a safe, alcohol-free environment. Not only do we want the teens to come and enjoy shows but also to show them that the community stands in support of their efforts."

Tony Lombardi says that the principal reason for initiating the Alex Gagnon Center was to provide an environment in which teenagers can develop their community responsibilities. He believes that music is the vehicle for achieving this.

Lombardi adds, "The kids will ultimately run the place themselves under a mentorship designed to teach how all this happens, rather than having to watch the show, then get up and leave." He continued, "The bottom line is to provide opportunities that you wouldn't normally have on an isolated island that may even stimulate future career choices for these kids."

Tony Peak plays the bagpipes at weddings, birthdays, memorials and special events. He learned to play with a local piper and piped through high school and college. For a while, he stopped playing but missed it and struggled to regain his earlier proficiency. He's been playing consistently for twenty-five years. A professional musician told him that for each day he fails to practice, it takes seven days to make it up. It's the physicality of playing, rather than the music that is the challenge.

Tony Peak enjoys general playing, and although he is not a virtuoso, he keeps up. "I've reached the level I want to be, playing for pleasure," he says. "I do enjoy it." Each year, Tony Pcak leads the opening march around the high school oval track in the annual Relay for Life walk to raise awareness and funds for the American Cancer Society. And in keeping with a Vineyard tradition, his daughter Barra played viola with the Vineyard Sinfonietta.

Chapter 11

MAYNARD PLAYED THE BLUES

Maynard Silva was "the Vineyard's homegrown, authentic American roots bluesman,"[77] known for "his National guitar, reedy harmonica, red high-top sneakers and growl of a voice."

Born in 1951, Maynard Silva grew up on the Vineyard, graduated from the regional high school in 1969, played the blues for forty years and died of cancer in 2008. His college roommate, Richard Brandenburg, paid the ultimate tribute: "Maynard Silva was the real deal. He lived his whole life inside the genius of the blues, because he fit it perfectly."

It was his English teacher, Leroy Hazelton, who introduced Maynard Silva to the blues. Another influence was the boogie-woogie piano playing of Gene Baer, his art teacher. When he first heard the blues, Maynard told the *Gazette* in 1987, "[Howlin'] Wolf's blues was so intense it scared me."

Petronio (Peter) Ortiz, an Island sign-painter,[78] encouraged Maynard to take up a side-line business, one that paid more reliably than music. As a teenager, Silva apprenticed with Ortiz and learned to eyeball a sign to get it right. "He was a great sign painter," said Jimmy Burgoff, a fellow musician. "I had him paint my truck. His sign-painting was considered good luck."

Maynard spent time in college in St. Louis and then drifted down to Memphis with his guitar, where he played with Bukka White. Paul Butterfield's slow blues made a strong impression on Silva, who measured success not by fame or fortune but by "keeping the pure American blues

sound alive, and of being able to hold his own on stage with people like Buddy Guy."[79] Working with Maynard was an honor. "Maynard was a bluesman for sure," said Jimmy Burgoff.

Over the years, Maynard played with such luminary bluesmen as Rick Danko and J.B. Hutto. He was on the road until the 1980s but returned to the Vineyard, saying, "It's depressing to be on stage in a bar at Christmastime."

Session guitarist Al Shackman remembered his friend: "He was like a throwback. I came to have the highest respect for him and put him on the same platform with those other bluesmen. He had it and there won't be another one coming along very soon, if ever."

Maynard married Island artist Basia Jaworska and kept playing even after diagnosed with cancer in 2005. In response to a musical fundraiser, Maynard thanked supporters: "For me, the best thing was still the music. Hearing people who I've watched study music for decades cut loose and play it real not only packed the dance floor but warmed my heart." He thanked everyone "for the spirit."

College roommate Richard Brandenburg recalled, "When I met him, he was a philosophy major already [at nineteen] steeped in the blues of being a Portuguese (Portugee) from Vineyard Haven." Silva was

Session guitarist Al Shackman, in his eighties, continues to play. *Courtesy of Dan Waters.*

Opposite: Of Maynard Silva, musician Jimmy Burgoff says, "He always treated his audience very well. He was a real gentleman. He was a great man." Jeremy Jones (left) with Maynard Silva. *Courtesy of Joyce Dresser.*

knowledgeable about Cape Verdean Morna music and Fado, Portuguese music from the 1820s. He celebrated black American blues.

"He was a wolf in every sense of the word at one time or another," said Laurel Redington of WMVY at the memorial for Maynard Silva after his death. "He is about this world experience, raw, on-the-toes reaching-for-the-heavens kind of music."

Johnny Hoy came to the Vineyard in a boat that sank, and "we were stuck with all our stuff and lived under the Big Bridge." Hoy was apprehended by the police and admonished by a judge to get a job. It was "destiny." Johnny says he loves the Vineyard because "I can always find work here. I always eat good."

His mother was a folk singer; his father followed the Clancy Brothers. "I like the big beat, and blues had that the best," he says. He also enjoys rock-and-roll, country and Cajun and learned from the records of Muddy Waters and James Cotton.

Keyboardist Jeremy Berlin tells how he joined Johnny Hoy and the Bluefish: "I sat in with Johnny at a wedding in 1993. That was the beginning. He invited me to various gigs over the summer and would pay me to come and play. Piano adds texture. At the end of the summer, I said, 'Am I in the band or not?' And he said, 'Yeah, you want to go to Maine tomorrow?'" Johnny Hoy and the Bluefish have regular gigs off-Island. That's how it began for Jeremy Berlin.

A couple years later, they were on the road and Berlin heard a record by guitarist William Buck. "Literally, my playing changed over night," he says. "I've learned the language, the secret code." He adds, "Most important: don't get in the way of the vocal. For a long time, I would play too much around the vocal. That is critical, learning to play less."

Jeremy Berlin plays most of the Bluefish gigs, with exceptions for touring with other bands. He has a keen perception of the performance. "People will come up and say you sound better than ever," he says. "They're so happy to have this moment, when you connect with them, and they're giving a little back to you, saying, 'Thank you. You made my life a little better.'"

"We're just a small fish in a small pond," says keyboardist Jeremy Berlin, but "you're having an impact on the next generation." *Courtesy of Jeremy Berlin.*

For a long time, Johnny Hoy was married, and his wife was the bass player in the band. When she and Johnny split, she left the band. Jeremy asked Johnny who would play bass. "Johnny said, 'You are, with your left hand,' and I said, 'OK,' and that's how I've become the bass player." Since then, he plays two parts, melody and bass. That sound has become part of the band.

"You have to feel the music," Jeremy Berlin says. "There are added pressures to always be consistent." The audience has certain expectations: "The pressure is on the musician every night to go out and deliver the goods. It doesn't matter if you feel like crap, if you have a cold or your wife just left you. It matters that you go out there and kick butt, the way mere mortals can't do it. A musician has to put himself on the line."

Johnny Hoy says people study musicians the way they're attracted to a fire: something special makes it work, a secret. He says, "I wanted what they had; I think I got it." *Courtesy of Jeremy Berlin.*

An exuberant audience appreciates Johnny Hoy and the Bluefish. *Courtesy of Jeremy Berlin.*

He says, "I am not a performer. That's not what I'm about. I'm just back here, making it happen. Performing is a very lonely and tough job."

Berlin speaks to the Vineyard music scene: "We've been doing this for thirty years. There's a generation of people [who] grew up with us for models of what's out there, for good or for bad. They start to go out to the Ritz, and there's Johnny Hoy and the Bluefish. They're starting to play and see us." He adds, "When they talk about influences, they talk about Johnny Hoy and Buck Shank. Take some of what you get and develop your own identity."

One night, Jeremy Berlin gave a budding musician a ride home; he now has a successful band. That ride "gave him a taste of what the feeling was. Being recognized." He adds, "We all have those moments. That's what growing up is. Take from your elders. You have to find inspiration somewhere."

Berlin talks of the next generation, making music: Willy Mason, Brad Tucker, Mike Parker, Chuck Stanwood and Adam Lipsky. Of the rock opera *The Ape Woman*, he observed, "The next generation [was] playing something really interesting. Adam Lipsky playing piano, playing jazz. When I heard him playing, he got it. It was a good lesson for me to let him learn his own way. You have to learn from the environment around you."

He reflects on his branch of the musical family tree. "There's a group of us, Tom Major and Mike Benjamin and Johnny Hoy and me, we're all getting up toward sixty. Everybody's still very active, going in the same direction as they always have, happily toiling away in whatever musical realm."

Al Shackman, in his eighties, played guitar with the greatest. Berlin says, "What I was doing impressed him. It's important to have someone else recognize me as a pianist. Everyone is playing for everyone else." That is the music community.

Chapter 12

VIBRANT VINEYARD VOICES

Barbara Lopes recalls sitting in the Federated Church in Edgartown, awaiting a performance by a high school group known as the Small Chorus. She suggested a new name: the Vineyard Minnesingers, which means "traveling musicians." "We were adamant we were not Minnisingers (little singers)," she says. "And Minnesingers topped the choice of 'Tom Grape and His Bunch.'"

"Tom" referred to Tom Mills, the instrumental and chorus teacher at the high school who formed the Small Chorus in 1967. Pam Butterick remembers him. He was an organist who "developed a terrific choir, and that genre has remained important to much of the island community." She says, "He was an exquisite director." Two dozen students were invited to that first group, and many are still on-Island.

The Vineyard Minnesingers first traveled through New England in 1968. They performed at St. John the Divine Cathedral in New York City, with Nancy Rogers on the cathedral organ. Pam Butterick recalls, "Possibly the most heartwarming memory is in the snack-room on the *Islander*, singing our a cappella repertoire of spirituals, such as 'Elijah Rock.' We sang all the way across the Sound, and were met by fire trucks and police cars celebrating this first Minnesinger tour." She adds, "This was truly a thrill for an Island girl in the '60s."

Rehearsals at Molly McAlpin's home on West Chop were memorable. "She paid for our first-ever uniforms, green jumpers and vests," says Pam. Her memories are specific: "We did so much classical choral music,

The first half of the Minnesingers program "is assembled in a serious setting," but then "letting loose in the second half, people wonder if it's the same kids," says director Janis Wightman. *Photograph by Thomas Dresser.*

some with piano, some with organ, some a cappella. For me the most memorable was 'Have Ye Not Known' and 'Ye Shall Have a Song.' Eight part a cappella, and thrilling to sing."

Kenny Ivory recalled the weekly rehearsals and the New York concert as highlights of his high school career. "It gave those of us who wanted a chance to expand our talent," adds Barbara Lopes. "Minnesingers was one of those experiences that make your high school years memorable."

When Tom Mills retired, Bob Nute became director. Barbara says, "He pushed us hard but made it fun. We sang on the freight deck of the *Islander.*" Nute introduced elements of a dance routine to balance the choral segment.

Janis Wightman is the current Minnesinger director. "I fell into it naturally," she says. She relishes how the students "start off. They like to sing, and they go off with lifelong friendships." As students improve, Ms. Wightman makes it "more challenging for them, they have to work harder." She loves "the feeling of accomplishment when it's finally over."

On alternate years, the Minnesingers travel abroad, an experience that "gives them a sense of being a citizen of the world," says Ms. Wightman proudly. "Our tour guide said we've changed the perspective of Americans overseas." They journeyed to Croatia in 2013 and Spain in 2015. "The last performance we did in Croatia, we went to sing to this little lady on a balcony. It was just for her. We were bringing her a gift."

Choral singing on the Vineyard has undergone several iterations since the 1960s, when the Martha's Vineyard Chorus was directed by Hamilton Benz. "The wonderful Harold Heeremans directed for several years," remembers Betsy Gately. "Harold was a white-haired ball of fire, a former professor of music, a great organist. I remember doing a Saint Saens piece with him, and also the 'Faure Requiem.'"

Born in Britain, Harold Heeremans retired in 1965 to Oak Bluffs. He oversaw church choirs at Trinity Methodist and the Old Whaling Church. "I faced, with a relaxed but adventurous spirit, two senior and two junior choirs, culminating in a Spring Concert by the combined senior choirs who thought they couldn't. I thought they could—they did," he wrote. This was retirement. "What a joy it was to enjoy music and, in the best sense of the word, play with it."[80]

What followed was the Abendmusik choir, directed by David Hewett. Abendmusik (German for "evening music") was smaller, recalls Glenn Carpenter, with good singers. "We did Bach and a lot of serious music but evolved into just a Christmas 'Messiah' program. Abendmusik ended, and many members transitioned into the Island Community Chorus."

Under the direction of Peter Boak, the Island Community Chorus first performed a program at the dedication of the new synagogue for the Martha's Vineyard Hebrew Center in 1996. The chorus sang the inaugural concert of the Performing Art Center (PAC) at the high school in 1997.

Monday evening rehearsals are when the chorus gets to work. "A lot of it [rehearsal] depends on the repertoire. Whatever we happen to be working on at the time seems to be my favorite." Boak goes on, "Many people come and want to sing and learn a solid piece of music." If the piece is too difficult, members self-select or weed themselves out. "You

The Island Community Chorus rehearses at the Trinity Methodist Church. Garrett Brown is the accompanist. *Courtesy of Nis Kildegaard.*

Monday night rehearsals for the Island Community Chorus are an integral part of the commitment to singing. *Courtesy of Nis Kildegaard.*

Conductor Peter Boak at work. *Courtesy of Nis Kildegaard.*

have to be careful that you don't damage the group as a whole for one person," Boak says.

"The more I work with them, the more I know how to get them to sing the way I want them to. What's really been fun to watch," he says, "as the chorus has evolved over the years, is to see how they've become so much more demanding of themselves."

The chorus offers three concerts a year: opening the summer season at the Tabernacle in early July, a holiday performance at the Old Whaling Church in December and a spring concert.

Mr. Boak has not shied from challenging his charges, who range in age, experience and ability. They number between 100 and 130 and delight in singing opera, show tunes and choral selections. The poetry of Russ Hoxsie provided lyrics for an original piece, "Road Sense," set to music by Island composer Philip Dietterich in 2006. Twice, the chorus has undertaken an ambitious Mendelssohn concert, *Elijah*, in 2008, with a twenty-four-piece orchestra, and *St. Paul*, in 2014. "The challenge," says Boak, "is to get everyone in the performance space, where they can see and hear and feel comfortable."

Jenny Friedman sings at the annual Reflections of Peace Christmas concert, which benefits Hospice of Martha's Vineyard. She sings with the Island Community Chorus, sometimes as a soloist. She is one of four members of the Union Chapel choir. "I guess you could say that I found my voice on Martha's Vineyard," she says. "Before I moved here I sang with a small, professional vocal ensemble. Boston is a very musical city, saturated with great singers, so I was content to be a conscientious ensemble member, a worker bee, happy to leave the solos to those bigger and better voices. Being a little fish in a big pond meant I had the chance to sing with many accomplished musicians, but because they did most of the heavy lifting, it also meant I got a bit lazy."

She continues:

> *All that changed when I moved to Martha's Vineyard in 2009. I was asked to become a soloist, sometimes with music I didn't think I could handle. I was faced with a choice: I could tell the people making these requests I had no business singing such music or I could step up, stretch myself, and see what my voice could do. I chose the latter, and I worked hard.*
>
> *As a result, I've found I can sing things I'd never imagined and discovered a voice I never knew I had. Ironically, this little island pond has given me more room to grow than that big pond in Boston.*

Island a Cappella began in 1990 as a madrigal group. The six men and six women took their music very seriously. "We did a lot of really serious and difficult modern jazz, madrigals and a lot of spirituals and gospels," recalls Glenn Carpenter. "We had a huge repertoire from all periods, all genres of music. It was a commitment; we did three or four concerts a year. Sang at a cocktail party for Bill Clinton in 1993." Island a Cappella disbanded in 1999. "Basses are a dime a dozen," notes Carpenter, a bass himself. "Good tenors are hard to find."

Vineyard Sound has become a fixture of Martha's Vineyard summer entertainment since it was formed in 1992. This all-male a

Vineyard Sound has become a fixture of the summer music scene on Martha's Vineyard. *Courtesy of Alison Shaw.*

cappella group of ten college students spends the summer singing on the Vineyard. Their repertoire ranges from traditional to classic, from Beatles to current radio hits.

Students from three Connecticut colleges shared a common love of music and the Vineyard. Jody Alford, of the first group, recalled, "We sang on the streets of Edgartown. One night we talked to the Navigator [now Atlantic] manager, and he said, 'Oh, now we can't use you.' So we started singing outside anyway and attracted a big crowd."[81]

Tom Dunlop noted, "They walked and sang their way like warbling Pied Pipers through town an hour before each concert, drawing parents and children and young women (and, occasionally, their reluctant-looking boyfriends) to the show."

"They know they're hokey," wrote Dunlop. "To stand up every night in a Vineyard Vines uniform of khaki shorts, bright Oxford shirt, printed tie, and flip-flops and sing with no instruments between you and your audience but a tuning fork, you'd pretty much have to be."[82] David Baker, of Vineyard Sound, says, "We're singing songs that both parents get and performing songs that kids get. That's really important." Vineyard Sound performs as many as eighty concerts each summer.

Ethan Underhill of Vineyard Sound sees the Vineyard as "a place for pleasure with elbow grease, where many people work hard" during the day to perform at night. He is part of something larger than himself, part of a tradition. Coming to the Vineyard, there's "some sort of magic when we step off the ferry, a spring in the step, a mystique."

Two Vineyarders who participated in Vineyard Sound over the years are Elijah Carroll and Chris Bettencourt. Elijah said, "You had to really care about each other and care about the group enough to invest yourself in it." Ivy Ashe reported, "Passing the torch to well-known friends keeps the group close-knit." Their way of keeping the group going is for the retiring man to pass on the opportunity to join the group to a talented friend.

Vineyard Sound records its performances at the Tabernacle and the Old Whaling Church and produces an album to preserve their special summer songs each year. The annual reunion concert draws veterans of previous years, all singing in harmony and having a good time doing it.

Chapter 13

VINEYARD JAZZ AND SOUL

John Alaimo first came to the Vineyard in 1972, part time, to play the Seaview; he moved on-Island in 1994. He has played at Wintertide, weddings and restaurants like the Edgartown Yacht Club. The duo of John Alaimo, with Mike Tinus, performs at Farm Neck and Atria. Sometimes Taurus Biskis plays drums. John Alaimo has performed at the Union Chapel, the Playhouse and the Whaling Church. He plays keyboard at big functions, though he prefers smaller sites.

Excitedly, he recalls a stint at the Vineyard Playhouse: "I was in *Billy Holliday* at Emerson's Bar and Grill. I played the piano, but the director, Marla Blakey, kept sneaking lines to me. It was just actress April Armstrong and me."

John Alaimo has nine albums of his recorded jazz. "It's me and Mike Tinus; Jeremy [Berlin] and Eric [Johnson] work together, and I fill in when Jeremy's busy. We are the jazz guys on the Island, the real stuff."

For years, John Alaimo played with Jimmy Burgoff, a former Islander who offered a few words on his Vineyard days. One time, "I was called at the last minute to play with Billy Eckstine and his pianist at a private party for the Duke Ellington Society in Oak Bluffs."[83]

Jimmy B is not above dropping a name or two. "One memorable cocktail party was at Lillian Hellman's home. The guests were happy doing a sing-along with us. Among the guests were Walter Cronkite, Beverly Sills, Mike Wallace, Art Buchwald and spouses." The stories

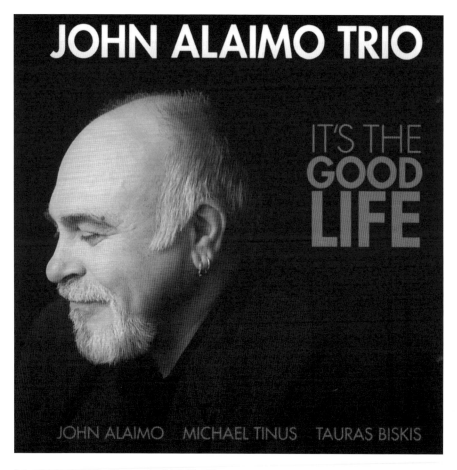

John Alaimo recalls, "I started with Mike Tinus about fifteen years ago. He plays bass, I'm on keyboard." Taurus Biskis plays drums in the trio. *Cover courtesy of John Alaimo.*

continue: "Ed Wise and I played an annual cocktail party at Robert McNamara's home on the south side of Edgartown."

Jeremy Berlin started in jazz, listening to be-bop, learning from Charlie Parker and Mingus and Monk records. He traces his interest in jazz to a radio special on Oscar Peterson. Attending a performance of Taj Mahal at Carly Simon's was impressive. "I wept," he says. "Music came from every pore in his body…He didn't need anyone else to play with him. He had it all: most importantly rhythm and time."

Jeremy Berlin has played jazz on the Island since 1983. Whenever time and circumstance allow, he is eager to play with other Island bands.

Four people exemplify mainstream jazz on the Vineyard: Jeremy Berlin, Eric Johnson, John Alaimo and Mike Tinus. "It's a very small little jazz world," says Berlin, who often plays with Eric Johnson. By playing with another talented musician, "We're very lucky to work as we do, in every gig that we do, and be able to advance our cause." They challenge one another to improve.

"You're putting yourself on the line every single time you play," he says. "When I sit down at the Ritz to play my music, I want it to sound good to me. I want it to sound good to my colleagues. And I want it to sound good to the people."

Blind from birth, David Crohan began to play the piano at the age of three. He attended the Perkins School for the Blind in Boston, where classical music was encouraged. After studying at the New England Conservatory of Music, he played recitals, chamber music performances and concerto appearances with symphony orchestras.

David Crohan visited the Vineyard in the summer of 1963, when he and his parents breakfasted at Mary's Restaurant, across from the Boston House, on Circuit Avenue. The regular pianist failed to show up that day, and David took over playing the piano in 1964. He met and jammed with Jose Feliciano and graciously took him out to dinner. That was shortly before Feliciano played at the Newport Folk Festival.

"David was good friends with George Munroe, who ran the Boston House. Munroe hosted the Jabberwocky kids at the Boston House, and David always played the piano," says Judy Williamson, one of the waitresses at the time. "The Boston House was the most popular restaurant on the Island." She adds, "David Crohan was such a presence at the Boston House."

A story shared with Linsey Lee of the Martha's Vineyard Museum relates to David Crohan's status as an Island celebrity in the late 1960s. While hitchhiking, he was picked up by a couple who recognized him. They complained that their teenagers, and one son in particular, were too interested in music. The parents worried there was no future in it. David said, "If he's good enough, he'll make it. But if he doesn't, he'll still have a rich life." The couple turned out to be the parents of James Taylor.

In 1978, David Crohan opened David's Island House on Circuit Avenue, "which rapidly became a magnet for music lovers who came to hear David's fascinating performances of both classical and jazz repertoire," according to his website. In 1990, he entertained Rose Fitzgerald Kennedy on her 100th birthday. David maintains a strong interest in jazz and has an amazing capacity to bridge boundaries between classical and jazz, as well as popular music.

His performances on the Vineyard are always well attended. In July 2014, his seventieth birthday concert filled the Tabernacle, much to the pleasure of his loyal fans. Patsy Costa, an ardent local supporter, said she was so grateful to attend the concert. For more than half a century, David Crohan has symbolized the magic and majesty of music on Martha's Vineyard.

Jim Thomas of the United States Slave Spiritual Choir learned slave songs from his great-grandmother, who was born a slave. He listened to spirituals in church, where he sang them as a child. Thomas grew up in Tennessee and attended Fisk University.

Thomas was a student of professor John W. Work III, director of the Fisk Jubilee Singers. Work's grandfather arranged many of the slave spirituals. The first John W. Work interviewed former slaves, uncovered primary sources and, in 1915, published *Folk Song of the American Negro*. He preserved Negro spirituals.

Regarding the Jubilee Singers, author Andrew Ward says, "At first they didn't include [spirituals] in their performances at all, until the day in 1872 when they straggled up to Oberlin, Ohio, and captivated a congress of Congregational ministers with an impromptu rendition of 'Steal Away.' That was when their conductor, George White,[84] first recognized the power of spirituals among white audiences, and the singers began collecting and arranging spirituals everywhere they went, including 'Swing Low,' 'Deep River,' and many more."[85]

Today, the a cappella Fisk Jubilee Singers are world-renowned.

"There has not been a new spiritual since [the Civil War]," says Jim Thomas. "They were created for the conveyance of secret messages. There was no need to do that after the war." Approximately one thousand

Of his United States Slave Spiritual Choir, Jim Thomas says, "No one else is doing this, not the way we do it." *Courtesy of Jim Thomas.*

spirituals are registered and digitalized in the Library of Congress. Some meanings or codes have been lost over the years; some songs have multiple verses or versions, while some songs are fragments.

"I love people to ask, 'With all the codes, how were they able to spread the codes across the land?'" says Thomas, with bemusement. The answer is slaves were sold, and the songs went with them. Word spread.

Jim Thomas opens his programs with the song "There's a Meeting Here Tonight." The late Pete Seeger introduced spirituals to the Civil Rights movement. Some spirituals were amusing, for example, "You may be a good Baptist or a good Methodist as well, but if you're not pure of heart, you're surely going to hell." Thomas adds, "Some songs were descriptions of life as a slave."

People confuse gospels with spirituals. Spirituals are old, undocumented and constitute a body of true American folk songs. The blues originated in spirituals. Gospels were consciously composed in the 1920s and '30s, first by Thomas Dorsey, a black man from Georgia. Gospels are composed in major keys and combine religious piety with rhythms associated with jazz and the blues.

Some of the thirty-plus members have been in the Slave Spiritual Choir since Jim Thomas founded it in 2004. No auditions are required. "I have some people that have real pitch problems," he says. "No one is to be excluded." The Spiritual Choir performs across Martha's Vineyard and off-Island. As a nonprofit, donations are directed toward transportation fees.

Inspiring his choir, Jim Thomas says, "I ask them to sing with passion. I start it, and they talk about it. Once they get it, it's a different song." He speaks of our common past, our common destiny. The past relates to slave masters who had children with slaves; the destiny is that now we're all in this world together. Thomas teaches his choir, his audience and his world about getting along, understanding and appreciating the lives and experiences of those who came before.

Chapter 14

THE ENERGY OF MUSIC

My grandfather Philip Mosher, the photographer, played the banjolele (ukulele/banjo hybrid)," Martha Child remembers. She bought a ukelele and, in 2012, formed a group with like-minded musicians. They perform locally, from libraries to senior centers and once outside Rocco's Pizza.

Martha says, "You have to understand that musicians never really like to give it up. When you're fifty-plus, the limelight sometimes passes you by or doesn't shine as brightly as it once did, so you must find a venue." Many are drawn to hits of the '20s, '30s and '40s. "Combine the two, and you have Vintage Voices."

Vintage Voices performs in venues similar to the Ukelele Band. Co-directors Mary Jean Miner and Phil Dietterich "work tirelessly to get the best performance we can with a combination of great music choices/arrangements and superb direction," says Martha Child. The goal is "to offer high-quality music to audiences who can't run to a concert hall. We like to think we cheer people up and lighten the loads of life. [Music] is the universal language."

Treble voices sang "Mr. Sandman," and lower voices sang "Sunrise, Sunset," in a version arranged by former Minnesinger Dorian Lopes. "Every effort is made to pretend each program is strung together in some sort of logical manner," smiles Mary Jean. "Phil Dietterich is our intrepid director and accompanist. He keeps us on our toes and is eternally

"We call ourselves the Princess PooPooly Ukelele Band after the 1938 song "Princess PooPooly Has Plenty Papaya (and She Loves to Give It Away)," says Martha Child, with Betsy Gately (left). *Courtesy of Joyce Dresser.*

encouraging," she says. "We have always said that when it stops being fun, we will stop. We sing unless specifically asked not to."

The seventy-year history of the Sinfonietta is fraught with gaps and revivals. The small group of woodwinds and strings has undergone cyclical changes in its long tenure. Established in 1946 by Island conductor Rudy Friebich, the Sinfonietta flourished for a few seasons and then took a hiatus through the 1950s. Allen Hovey revitalized the group in a concert in 1961. Heidi Schultz, of that incarnation, still participates in today's Sinfonietta, playing cello and arranging the music on her Finale program, which honors the original mission to "encourage amateur musicians to practice and perform music on their various instruments (strings and winds) for the public benefit." It is an incorporated nonprofit.

Edie Yoder expanded the repertoire of the Vineyard Sinfonietta when she took over as conductor, and the group grew to thirty musicians. This was 1995. *Courtesy of Edie Yoder.*

Vineyard Sinfonietta performing in 2014. *From left to right*: Edie Yoder, Heidi Schultz and Jessica Roddy. *Courtesy of Thomas Dresser.*

Tom Mills worked for the school system in the 1960s and was hired to conduct both the Vineyard Chorus and the Vineyard Sinfonietta. The Sinfonietta flourished under Mills, who incorporated students in joint concerts with the Chorus and Sinfonietta, from 1963 to 1967. Of his final concert, Mills noted, "Not terribly exciting but well performed."

Another notation in the files of the Sinfonietta reads: "In 1967 I started a select high school chorus as part of my teaching program." What began as the Small Chorus evolved into the Minnesingers.

After several seasons, the Vineyard Sinfonietta slipped into hibernation for more than a dozen years. In the early 1980s, it was revived by Hamilton Benz, who offered programs in conjunction with Harold Heereman's Chorus. A memorable performance at David's Island House in 1983 featured David Crohan performing a Mozart piece and the Vineyard Sinfonietta playing Bach.

The Sinfonietta languished again, "ebbing and flowing like the tides around us," as the saying goes. In 1993, Ray Kellman revived it. Mezzo-soprano Martha Hudson joined the Sinfonietta as a vocalist in 2005, adding depth to the sounds of the strings.

The Vineyard Sinfonietta has invited high schoolers to Sinfonietta concerts and held joint concerts with the high school orchestra. In high school, Barra Peak played viola with the Sinfonietta and was highly respected by her musical peers, one of whom was seventy years her senior.

"In its present incarnation," says Edie Yoder, "the Vineyard Sinfonietta has one high schooler and eight to ten adult string players who meet Sunday afternoons for love of the music from our well-stocked music library [128 orchestral and chamber music parts]."

Founded in 1971, the Martha's Vineyard Chamber Music Society (MVCMS) is firmly woven into the Island's musical heritage. Because of MVCMS, residents and visitors with tastes for the classics and progressive music have them available. Longtime artistic director Dee Stevens brings sterling musicians from across the country to present five memorable music programs twice a week during the summer music festival, as well as Thanksgiving and spring programs.

Chamber music is an intimate performance by a small group of players, usually fewer than nine, who perform with no conductor. Even for the uninitiated, the music impresses. Chamber music varies from traditional to modern, from jazz to classical.

The origins of MVCMS began on the West Coast with a trio composed of clarinetist John Gates; his wife, cellist Caroline Worthington; and Delores Stevens, a concert pianist. They performed as the Montagnana Trio and traveled in the States and Europe. In 1971, Eleanor Piacenza, Caroline's mother and, incidentally, Thomas Hart Benton's mother-in-law, invited them to the Vineyard to play for Tisbury's tercentennial at the Katharine Cornell theater.

The group found a demographic underserved by classical music and moved east with their music to fill the void. The evolution of the Montagnana Trio into the Martha's Vineyard Chamber Music Society was pure Vineyard. Dee Stevens said, "It just feels right to make such beautiful music in such a wonderful place."

Of the Vineyard Strings, flutist Edie Yoder says, "What began in 1985 has now over 150 K-8 string music students and a thriving high school orchestra." *Courtesy of Edie Yoder.*

Initial performances were outdoors, as afternoon musicales. The first indoor concert was at what became home for the MVCMS: the Chilmark Community Center, which was offered without charge by the center's then president, Rosemary Clough. Trio performances were conducted in the round, on the floor. Jim Norton provided a piano. Financial support was generated by an activist board headed by Ray Kellman, while housing and rehearsal space was provided by Eleanor Piacenza.

The trio broke up in 2001, leaving its artistic director, Dee Stevens, on her own. Growing up in the Depression, she recalls she sang for the Civilian Conservation Corps, and "I found myself a job as accompanist in the local Methodist church, but I was fired. I played too fast. Those Methodists moved very slowly."[86]

Fine musicians are attracted to the Vineyard. They come, it is said, for the beach, for the lobster and for the congeniality of hospitality offered by board members. These virtuosos include major orchestra first chairs, sought-after soloists and those who are masters of exotic instruments (for this culture), like the marimba. Even today, the Martha's Vineyard Chamber Music Society operates on a tight budget, dependent on donors to sponsor concerts.

Paul Stevens, Dee's son, has recruited fellow graduates of the Juilliard School. The Chamber Music Society continues to thrive, retaining Dee's commitment to bringing world-class music to the Vineyard. Dee says, "Attendance at our concerts hasn't declined. People yearn to be lifted out of their daily lives."[87]

The chamber's mission is "to produce chamber music concerts, promote and support classical music learning opportunities, especially for our local schools." Edie Yoder explains, "In 1985, president Ray Kellman was instrumental in providing instruments for some children and adults." Kellman, along with Heidi Schultz and Edie Yoder, of the Sinfonietta, established "a community-based string education program."

The Chamber Music Society induced Nancy Jephcote and Jonathan Beach to teach. Edie Yoder continues: "The MVCMS lobbied the school committee for this inclusion into the MV Public School Music Department because string instrument training had been cut from the budget."

The *Vineyard Gazette* noted, "The program is free for all students and they can rent their instruments from the program or purchase their own. Financial help is available, made possible in part by the Martha's Vineyard Chamber Music Society." Strings reentered the elementary extracurricular program in 1988; Nancy Jephcote, of the Flying Elbows, became full-time instructor in 2002.[88]

The Long Point Five "is an experienced and whimsical group of Island musicians who enjoy sharing music with their community."[89] The range of members is impressive, and they play a variety of music, from classics to jazz.

The Long Point Five evolved from friendships formed in the Vineyard Haven Band. It started in 2011, with John Schilling on trumpet, Jim Athearn on trombone, Julie Schilling on clarinet, Bud Larson on flute and Jeri Larson on piano. "We're all seasoned musicians without big egos," Jeri Larson said. "We thought it would be fun to 'play out,' and we began doing that a couple of years ago."

They perform at local libraries and senior centers. "We get a kick out of watching ninety-year-olds get up and dance and clap their hands to their favorite music like Gershwin and Scott Joplin," Ms. Larson said.

The quintet has "such a good time together; we'd love to have other opportunities for Island people to hear us."

Merrily Fenner says her most wonderful musical moment was at a nursing home years ago, where her aunt was a resident. She was playing guitar with Mark Mazer, "and this woman wobbled over and mouthed the words of the song we were singing. The staff was amazed because the woman had been mute for ten years," Merrily pauses. "Music has a way of bringing back the memories, especially when old songs are sung."

Her group, Serendipity, began by singing at Joy Flander's funeral. "We wanted something good to come of it. We like doo-wop; we had a guitar player and a good singer and said, 'We can do it.'" Merrily adds, "We feel so blessed we're doing it." With a repertoire of more than one hundred songs, they are well ensconced in the Vineyard music scene, performing at the Wharf, the PA Club and benefits across the Island.

Years ago, Merrily played in the Stragglers, with John Early and Danny Whiting. Now she entices Nancy Jephcote and Hugh Taylor to play with Serendipity. She opens for David Crohan, having spent nine years playing at David's Island House. "He is such a wonderful man. We have a ball with him," she says. "He always donates to Camp Jabberwocky."

Of Mark Mazer, she says, "Mark and I go way back. Mark is more of a country guy; I taught him when he was a kid. I asked him if he wanted to learn the old standards in the Stragglers, and he did." Mark was invited to join Serendipity when a key member of the group passed away.

Merrily Fenner's musical past includes a stint at the Tivoli in the early 1960s. Her father was Hamilton Benz, who invigorated the Sinfonietta and conducted the Martha's Vineyard Chorus in the late 1960s; he played with Gale Huntington. The musical heritage runs strong and deep in the chords of Merrily's guitar.

One of the constants in the history of music on Martha's Vineyard, older than any other musical ensemble, is the Vineyard Haven Band. In the latter part of the twentieth century, the Vineyard Haven Band adapted to changing times, inviting woodwinds and women to join and naming its first female president, who eventually became conductor of the band. Julie Schilling was named the first female president of the band in 1981, in charge of musicians who ranged in age from eleven to seventy. In 1984, the band had eighty members but was still short a tuba and trombone player; a later plea sought a clarinetist.

In 1993, the band commemorated the centennial of Katherine Lee Bates's "America the Beautiful." It recognized the 300th anniversary of Chilmark in 1994 and honored Gale Huntington. The next year, the group hailed World War II vets on the 50th anniversary of VJ Day. Julie Schilling stepped in as substitute conductor in 1995.

The public was "invited to come, enjoy the breezes and the view of the Tisbury harbor scene as the Vineyard Haven Town Band serenades you." *Gazette* reporter Maeve Reston mentioned how musicians spanned the generations.

An editorial by Henry Beetle Hough portrayed the band as an essential part of summer: "Band concerts are an institution which we hope will never change." The band is a "great asset to the Island. Thousands of people enjoy hearing it play. Summer is really summer when the band begins to play in the open and the whole family settles down, upon the grass or upon seat cushions to enjoy the luxury of listening."[90] The spirit of the band lives on, pounding out familiar tunes summer after summer, keeping tradition alive as it has over the past 150 years.

Edson Rogers plays trumpet with the Vineyard Haven Band. As a youngster growing up in Vineyard Haven, he recalls the band marching down Franklin Street in a parade rehearsal: "My music teacher was Rudy Friebach. How fortunate was I to get started by him. I played in the Legion Drum and Bugle Corps, dances at the Legion Hall. It was a wonderful time." Ed Rogers knew Albert Huntington, Gale and Willie's brother, who played piano and arranged pieces for the Legion.

After thirty years as trumpet instructor with the Navy Band, Ed Rogers was pleased and proud to invite the Northeast Navy Band to march through Vineyard Haven to re-dedicate Veterans Field and to play a free concert at the Tabernacle on Flag Day in 2014. What a treat to hear him perform a solo in a selection with the Navy Band.

Edson Rogers plays at the Vineyard Haven Memorial Day celebration and occasional weddings. He says it is a privilege when he is asked to play at a veteran's funeral.

Chapter 15

AND THE ANGELS SING

The Daytrippers evolved from a 2011 spring musical called *OBeatles* at the Oak Bluffs Elementary School, directed by Shelagh Hackett and produced by music teacher Brian Weiland. That auspicious concert involved students of all grade levels singing and acting out Beatles songs. Since then, the Daytrippers evolved into a popular band, playing the Beatles with attention to detail that lends their concerts an authenticity appreciated by fans of all ages.

Boaz Kirschenbaum is the man behind the Daytrippers, which is neither a cover band nor a tribute band. "I guess we are 'stewards' of the Beatles' recorded music," he says. "We study the recording processes, the gear, the mixes, the instrumentation, as though we are musicologists. We study the Beatles' music the way classical musicians study 'performance practice' of Mozart or Beethoven. Mostly, though, we try to have a great time playing songs with all our friends. We love the Vineyard, and the Beatles' music struck a chord here."

"The six-member group is composed principally of Vineyard teachers and musicians who jammed together and had a 'what if…' moment a year ago," wrote Jack Shea in the *Martha's Vineyard Times* on April 9, 2012. "The result is a well-researched and orchestrated performance on '60s era instruments covering the mopheads' total body of work, including some never-performed pieces."

Because their concerts are infrequent, their aura reaches near mythical proportions. "The power of The Beatles music and times doesn't draw just those of, er, a certain age, but appeals to the full demographic: tykes to octos," added Shea. Fans of varied age and ilk express appreciation for the skillful styles and measured beat of the Daytrippers. Their renditions of Beatles songs propel hands to clap and feet to tap.

And the Daytrippers offer something besides music. They play for fundraising ventures such as Habitat for Humanity and the Island Grown Initiative and raised $3,000 toward a kitchen at the West Tisbury school.

To express his altruistic intent, Boaz Kirschenbaum celebrated his fortieth birthday on February 1, 2014, with a community concert at the Katharine Cornell Theatre, offering popular music ranging from the Grateful Dread (Mike Benjamin's tribute band) to the Flying Elbows, from Good Night Louise to, of course, the Daytrippers, all to raise funds for musical instruments for the Vineyard public schools.

Boaz said, "I really wanted to see if I could put on a concert for the community that was a real professional concert but with no money involved." Musicians and technical people donated their time for the rehearsals and the concert. That particularly defines the Daytrippers: they play purely for the pleasure of celebrating the community.

Shelagh Hackett sings lead vocals; other players include Doug Brush, Charlie Esposito, Eric Johnson and Brian Weiland, as well as Boaz Kirschenbaum.

And in the spirit of the Beatles' "All You Need Is Love," Boaz Kirschenbaum met Shelagh Hackett at the 2011 *OBeatles* program, and the two are to be married. With children from previous marriages, Boaz, a piano tuner by trade, says, "So we not only have a big family, but they are all musical. All of our children are huge Beatles fans and have been to almost all of our concerts."

REFLECTIONS OF A MUSIC MAN

Brian Weiland (rhymes with Island) came to the Vineyard in 1994; he was hired as the Oak Bluffs music teacher in 1998 and has found himself actively involved in many roles in the Vineyard music scene over the past twenty years.

Of Maynard Silva, Brian Weiland recalls, "[He was] a wonderful gruff character, the quintessential bluesman." Weiland was the drummer in Maynard's band for a while. One night, "between sets someone from one

Brian Weiland, musical chameleon, playing washboard with the Flying Elbows.
Courtesy of Dan Waters.

of the Island newspapers approached Maynard and asked if he minded pictures being taken. Maynard didn't even look up as he said, 'If I'd-a known you were comin', I'd-a brought a better lookin' band.'"

Weiland volunteered at Wintertide at Five Corners and recalls "seeing some amazing shows in exchange for working the front door." Meeting James Taylor at Wintertide was a "personal highlight."

Brian Weiland has been "Everyman" in the field of Vineyard music over the last two decades. Like Forrest Gump, he appears in many different settings, always producing, performing and pleasing his audience.

A list of his musical appearances includes a five-year stint with the Vineyard Haven Band. He often plays drums for the Island Community Chorus, led by his neighbor Peter Boak, and has participated in the Island Theater Workshop programs. For a couple years, he was in a trio at the Reflections of Peace concert with Nancy Jephcote and Steve Tully. Weiland is often called on to provide percussion with theatrical programs at the Katharine Cornell Theatre and the Vineyard Playhouse. He has played for Minnesinger concerts and traveled abroad with them to Ireland and Austria.

Brian Weiland is not averse to working with children: he assisted Taffy McCarthy in her teenage gospel choir and now oversees the music at the annual Christmas Eve children's program at the Agricultural Hall. For eighteen years, he has sung Christmas carols at the Oak Bluffs tree lighting.

He recorded with Kate Poole in a duo called Another Roadside Attraction, and he played classy jazz with Troy Tyson, adorned in a white dinner jacket with maroon bow tie. Weiland was one of the last to perform at the Hot Tin Roof and at David's Island House and one of the first to play at Offshore Ale, with theater director Taffy McCarthy.

Weiland recounts playing with McCarthy's teenage girls gospel choir at a benefit for the Vineyard Haven Library at Carly Simon's barn. Members of Aerosmith were in the audience, and Brian "slipped in the riff to 'Same Old Song and Dance,'" one of their early hits, which generated "a big smile, and cheer, and thumbs-up."

As a teacher, Brian Weiland offers guidance and direction to the next generation. "I ran an afterschool guitar class, and my very first students were Willy Mason and Sebastian Keefe, now very successful professional musicians," he says.

"Mr. Weiland's not great," confides seven-year-old Shealyn Smyth, her face brimming with portent. "He's awesome," she laughs. Shealyn has developed a deep appreciation for music from the teaching of Brian Weiland.

As an accompanist, Weiland "especially enjoyed playing for the high school because I could see and hear how far the students I had taught as small children had taken their talents."

Of his own children, his oldest, Liam, plays drums, cello, guitar, bass and sings in the Minnesingers. Daughter Avalon plays the Celtic harp, "and my youngest son, Aiden, is probably the most precocious musician.

Lenny Baker, saxophonist for Sha Na Na, played in Ray Frazio's band on the Vineyard. Brian Weiland played drums in Frazio's band; later, he played guitar and sang. *Courtesy of Alison Shaw.*

He has been playing fiddle since before he entered school." His children sometimes accompany him to renaissance fairs and music festivals.

Brian sings and plays acoustic guitar with Rick Bausman at Camp Jabberwocky. Bausman's son Hudson "provides the most funky rock-solid beats it has ever been my pleasure to play over."

As the "chameleon" of the Flying Elbows, Weiland finds the group is "one of the more interesting musical phenomena."

Weiland was instrumental in the formation of the Daytrippers, whose shows, he says, "have been among the most fun musical experiences."

On the future of Vineyard music, he says the "worst thing to happen to live music on the Island is the banning of outdoor music, first in Edgartown, and then Oak Bluffs." Curtailing live music "successfully killed all 'busking' in Oak Bluffs," which means no opportunity for public performances. (Busking is to play or perform in public, soliciting funds.)

Nevertheless, he says, "Being a music teacher on this island is the greatest job in the world. The arts here are incredibly valued, incredibly strong and vibrant." Understandably, his "biggest problem is that I have more offers to participate in musical activities than I have time for." He goes on: "Music is among the most joyful things we can do to both express our individuality, and to revel in our connectedness."

Jemima James is a singer/songwriter. For years, she worked in New York but now composes and performs on the Vineyard. She says, "To write, I need a room, a guitar, uninterrupted time."

She loves "any music that stops me thinking and gets me feeling." Jemima James says, "In the old days, it was the Wintertide at five corners, a great venue for kids and adults to play. My kids played there in their bands Slow Leslie and Keep Thinking."

She continues, "I love music parties where people are playing their latest songs, singing impromptu harmonies. One night a few of us wound up in the kitchen. Lexie Roth and Sam Mason improvised a fantastic, hilarious rap song while beating out the rhythm on the fridge" with spoons. "That Lexie and Sam rap song was a great memorable moment."

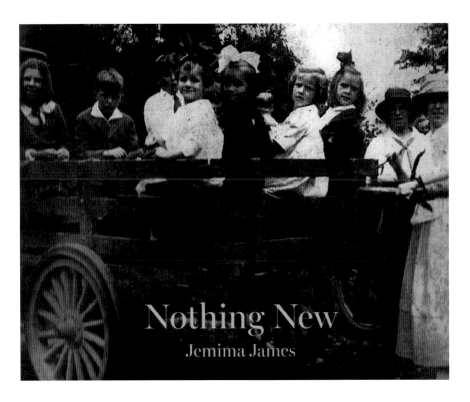

Nothing New
Jemima James

Jemima James finds that "the audiences on the Vineyard are alert and appreciative." *Courtesy of Dan Waters.*

Opposite: *Nothing New*, by Jemima James. The album blends country, folk, bluegrass and rock. Jemima's sons, Willy and Sam Mason, and her friends participated in the album. *Cover used with permission of Jemima James.*

Jemima James (pictured with Kate Taylor, on the left) says her favorite Vineyard venue is Featherstone Center for the Arts, at the Musical Mondays performance center. *Courtesy of Dan Waters.*

Jemima James recalls songwriter retreats at the Wintertide with Tony Lombardi, "who always rooted for me." The retreats included the likes of Tom Paxton, Jack Hardy, Christine Lavin and Dave Van Ronk. Jemima says she had "the good sense and courage to take a songwriting workshop with Bob Franke, who was a fantastic workshop leader, and right away a surprising, fresh song bubbled up. It helped bring me out of my overly precious songwriter shell."

She explores the challenge of writing: "At another retreat night of performances I sang two songs. I was scared and shaky. One of the songs I wrote was half in English and half Spanish, inspired by my love of mariachi music. I didn't pull it off very well, but after I sat back down, Tom Paxton came over and whispered in my ear, 'You're a strong writer; stick to what you know best.' He gave my shoulder a squeeze, very kind and supportive. I'll never forget it."

Jemima's son Willy Mason has made a name for himself in the music world: "Both my sons bring the big joy. Whatever they do, they work hard and they do it well." Sam works in New York as an artist, writer and drummer. Willy Mason's work "has grown exponentially since he went out on the road right out of high school." She looks back in time: "When the boys were young I called them the Amazin' Mazon Brothers. They had several bands with their friends that rehearsed in our basement: Slow Leslie, Keep Thinking, Howl." Nowadays she's proud that "Sam and Willy are contributing great things to the world, and they're making a living doing what they love. Beyond that, everything's gravy."

Chapter 16

ROCK ON

Mike Benjamin grew up in Cambridge, took up the guitar at thirteen and played the subway station at Harvard Square, busking for spare change. In 1970, he came to the Vineyard for the summer, camped in the woods and earned money playing guitar.

In the 1960s and '70s, the Seaview bar was rowdy and loud. Loretta Balla (1911–2010), the owner, was rough around the edges, yet she had a kind heart. "Anyone who remembers the Seaview knows it was a special place," says Mike Benjamin, who got his break there. "The vibe was amazing, like a funky bar, packed to the gills, floor disgustingly dirty."

In 1971, Mike assembled a band and rented an unfinished house in Chilmark. He circulated a press package but got no takers. One day, "Loretta Balla called up and said, 'Mike, you're playing here tonight.' We were ready. We had a five-piece band and about fifteen hangers-on," Mike recalls. They played the Seaview on Thursday, Friday and Saturday, and it proved profitable. Although he and his band were getting better all the time, Mike feared Loretta would fire him at any moment.

Mike Benjamin relocated to New York from 1985 to 1995, writing music for TV and radio, but visited the Vineyard each summer. In the twenty years since his return, he says, "I do weddings, and when I have a chance, I write. I do a lot of covers. I'm a working musician in other people's bands. I sub for people. I'm a music addict."

Mike was in the band Entrain and then began to work on his eponymous group and released two albums independently, *Never Too Late*

"Kevin Keady" by Allen Ginsberg, October 8, 1985. "He shaped my thinking and taught me how to play the piano," says Keady of Allen Ginsberg. Ginsberg inscribed the photograph: "Kevin Keady as he looked, handsome at the kitchen table—heroic even—but can he manifest it in the world of time?" *Courtesy of Kevin Keady.*

and *Backyard*. He is a founding member of the Grateful Dread, a tribute band with a faithful following.

Over the course of the one hundred days of summer, Mike Benjamin might perform as many as twenty weddings and dozens and dozens of bar gigs. Fellow musician Jeremy Berlin says, "Mike Benjamin has become a really good wedding band. He has gone from a very good bar-band guy, and a guy who writes great songs, to a very professional band, very complete, smart and thoughtful."

Martha's Vineyard is a prime wedding destination, and Mike Benjamin plays a lot of weddings. He says, "The fun part of a wedding, for me, is to try to mix it up. If the wedding is in a nice place, a lot of times I stretch my

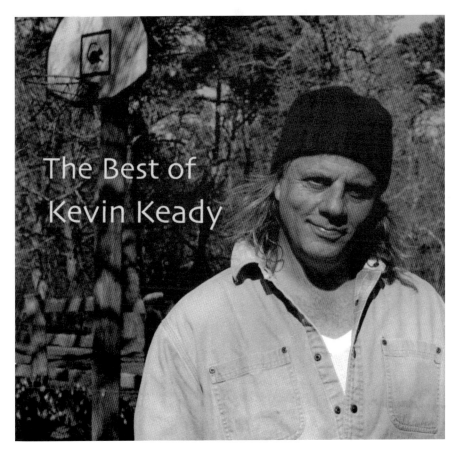

Kevin Keady, shown on this album cover, performs at the West Tisbury Farmers' Market, which generates a dozen or so gigs for him per summer. *Courtesy of Kevin Keady.*

abilities, play jazz, a mixed bag of different styles. It's a challenge I like." He plays with other local musicians Jeremy Berlin, Johnny Hoy and Kevin Keady and says, "I have enjoyed being here."

Another Vineyard singer/songwriter is Kevin Keady. He says, "I consider myself a songwriter and find the ultimate pleasure in performing original songs for a live audience. Everything else is a secondary way of achieving the goal of playing music, playing in public, connecting with people." Keady puts himself out there. He never thought he had the voice for singing other people's songs, "but after years of amassing a catalogue of cover songs that I truly love, it seemed like the natural progression."

The songs he sings are what make his group, Kevin Keady and the Cattledrivers, unique. Bearing a strong Americana influence, he chose a name that resonates with the country's rugged outdoorsmen.

For several years, Kevin Keady and the Cattledrivers have played the Farmers' Market in West Tisbury on Saturday mornings in season. He loves it. "It's a gig that suits my clothes and songs," he says. He also performs at Musical Mondays at Featherstone Center for the Arts. A few more singer/songwriter venues would be welcome, Kevin adds.

Kevin Keady had a long and impressive rapport with Allen Ginsberg. He was "a big fan of all things Dylan, Grateful Dead and beat." With a couple friends, he attended one of Allen Ginsberg's beat poetry readings and, in 1986, relocated to a farm Ginsberg owned.

Keady has had two songs printed in the *Martha's Vineyard Times*: "Hay Day," an homage to the work-a-day life on a hay farm, and "One Way Home (The Chappy Ferry Song)," in the *Chappy Ferry Book*.

"I have a lot of different bands because I like a lot of different music," says Don Groover. "I play Americana roots, rock, funk, blues. I just like to make noise."

Groover claims he has played the Ritz more than any other musician. It's his home base, and his is the house band. However, he is not content with a single band but coordinates or participates in half a dozen bands, depending on the venue. He is a regular with the Cattledrivers. And he plays in the Beetlebung Steel Band. Besides those, he says, "I'm in charge of myself and my bands, so I don't get into double bookings. A lot of musicians may forget or be late; one guy I called a half hour before a show, and he said, 'Was that tonight?'" He smiles, ruefully, "It's kind of like daycare, having a lot of children to take care of."

There was a time when Don Groover considered going on the road, but when his son was born, that convinced him to stay put. "Maybe that was the wrong choice," he says, "but I did it." Very rarely does he turn down a gig. "I manage to find people to do it. I like making noise, playing music." He has a few original songs, some recorded at a jam, and he covers other artists, but his primary goal is to make music.

And when someone from another band can't show up, if Don's free, he's there. He has such confidence and experience that he does not need to see what the band is playing. "I just fill in and ad lib the notes. That's my favorite thing to do. A lot of music follows a formula, so I know when a break is coming and anticipate the chord change."

At the age of thirteen, Groover got his first guitar and never looked back. He picked up the banjo a decade ago. He says, "I told my wife I was having a mid-life crisis; couldn't afford a Corvette so I got a banjo." Now he plays an hour or so in the morning before he heads off to his day job at the Tisbury Printer.

At Berklee College of Music, Don Groover studied big band arrangements, learning how different parts come together. Now he experiments with different chords to change a song and make it stand out.

Groover considers versatility his strength, along with reliability. "Never missed a gig in forty years," he claims. He was late once, when he got lost in South Boston, but on the Vineyard, he shows up early to get set up and tune up and anticipate the night ahead. Don Groover loves to make music and does it as often as possible.

Tom Major, son of a jazz drummer, has played drums since the age of five and been associated with many prominent musicians, including those in the band Magic Music. He was Bo Diddley's drummer, and it was during that incarnation in 1993 that he founded the popular band Entrain. According to the Entrain website, "[Major] is passionate about bringing Entrain's positive message of Peace, Love, Unity and a Greener World to its all age fan base, while having fun doing it."

Entrain's music is made by "mixing world influenced rhythms, pop song writing, and a positive upbeat vibe. Entrain was an instant hit and has been thrilling critics and fans of all ages." Tom Major says, "We want to create music that makes people feel good. When we look out from the stage, all we see is smiling faces of all ages and bodies moving. You can't beat that feeling. At the same time, if we can help to promote positive values and lifestyles, great! Let's spread a little joy around and watch how infectious it can be."

Joe Keenan offers his perspective on how the music scene has changed over the past thirty years. "I came to the island to play a benefit concert in 1987 and stayed. As fate would have it, I got a job on the *Shenandoah* as cook, and my focus changed. I am a singer/songwriter, and there have been few venues that support that genre. The Wintertide was the best place, but as it turns out, it wasn't sustainable."

To get accepted and appreciated as a musician is difficult. Some musicians manage to make it. For others, it is not so easy. Joe Keenan says, "The best thing about being a musician on the Island over the years is that most people are supportive in subtle ways. We have such a strong community of artists and artisans that people make room for the vagaries that accompany the drive to play out." Joe notes that when he works for a contractor and has to leave early for a gig, his boss has no problem letting him go. He adds, "It is the support we get from others that makes it possible for us to pursue our artistic endeavors." He says that accommodation has meant a great deal to him and to many others over the years.

Ann Smith, director of Featherstone Center for the Arts, hosts the popular summer music series Musical Mondays. She says, "Every carpenter on Martha's Vineyard is a wannabe musician, with a guitar in his pick-up truck, ready to play at a moment's notice."

Chapter 17

ALL ALONG THE STRINGED INSTRUMENT HIGHWAY

In the guitar community, Arlen Roth is "the guitar player's guitar player." He has backed-up, traveled with, recorded with and instructed many of the household names in the guitar community. Roth solos and records in the many genres of guitar playing. He created an innovative teaching technique that moved many players to higher performance levels. With the Internet, his teaching skills are accessible to the international guitar-playing community.

Living in Aquinnah, in the southwestern corner of Martha's Vineyard, Arlen Roth's interests extend beyond guitars. He has an impressive collection of automobiles and memorabilia, as well as vintage guitars. A comprehensive treatment of Arlen's many gifted contributions to the world of guitars appeared in the August 2008 issue of *Martha's Vineyard Magazine*:

> *Underlying it all seems to be Arlen's search for "soul," a feeling that pervades the collection and the music to which he has devoted his life: blues, country, folk, and rock—music that defines the soulful roots of America* [which seems to have congealed for him at Martha's Vineyard]. *It applies ultimately to Arlen himself, who in a world of fifteen-minute fame and disposable everything, truly values and works to preserve the American soul that remains.*

As with Carly Simon's and James Taylor's offspring, and so many others, Arlen's daughter, Lexie, now in her twenties, is a full-fledged singer/songwriter. She performs and records with her father and other dignitaries in the world of guitar. A look at the collaborations between them suggests a tight bond brought by the tragic car accident that claimed the lives of her stepmother and sister. She's an integral part of the up-and-coming Vineyard musical community.

A second stop on the "Stringed Instrument Highway," that long and winding roadway that links Vineyard musicians, is also in Aquinnah: the workshop and home of master craftsman Flip Scipio. "The names of Flip Scipio's clients—Paul McCartney, Bruce Springsteen, Bob Dylan, Jackson Browne, Ry Cooper, and Carly Simon among them—are testament to him as a guitar technician," wrote Mike Seccombe.[91]

Flip Scipio is a modest man, living and working in Aquinnah with his wife, bookbinder Mitzi Pratt. "What he mostly is, is the guitar fixer to the gods," wrote Seccombe. Scipio enjoys the process of repairing a guitar. He puts everything into the process, earning a reputation as a perfectionist.

Scipio's reputation was secured in 1993 when he repaired Paul McCartney's Hofner bass, the one he played with the Beatles. As Scipio recounted the tale to *Martha's Vineyard Magazine*, "It was an extraordinary, weird experience. They flew it over on the Concorde; it came with an armed guard, although I didn't know he was armed until later when someone said, 'Man he's a real tough guy, he's always got guns.'" For the duration of the time spent repairing the guitar—two days—the guard remained on site. Flip Scipio takes it all in stride: "Actually, I really had a nice time talking to him. He was a Cockney, smoked cigars, told great stories."[92]

Not only does he repair the guitars of the stars, but he also builds superb instruments. One of his first guitars has been played by such stars as Jackson Browne and Paul Simon. "Top-flight musicians look upon their guitars as tools. What they care about is the sound, not the look," Seccombe said.

A documentary about his work, *Talking Guitars*, explores his creative perfectionism, his methodical musical mien. Flip Scipio is a careful craftsman. And sometimes, he says, he repairs broken banjos.

Next stop is the Keith farm, near Beetlebung Corner, Chilmark. Bill Keith grew up in Boston but summered on the Keith farm in Chilmark. That's where he developed his mastery of the banjo. Dave Seward remembers, "He used to have a group, and they'd practice up on Middle

Road. That's where he honed his skill." As a teenager, Keith exhibited an interest in folk music, inspired by the likes of Pete Seeger and Earl Scruggs. At nineteen, Bill Keith performed at the Moon Cusser, prior to his national recognition as a master banjo player. He joined iconic Bill Monroe's bluegrass band and moved to Nashville.

Banjos played an integral role in folk music in the 1960s. Bill Keith garnered stature in modern banjo playing when he introduced his unique style of picking, known as the melodic or "Keith picking" style. This was allowed by his creation of the Keith tuning plug. He urged banjo players to play "newgrass," also known as progressive bluegrass, utilizing electric banjos and playing songs from other genres, such as rock-and-roll. Bill Keith continues to play and give seminars and banjo lessons in the States and abroad.

Another stop on the "Stringed Instrument Highway" is along Middle Road, north of the Keith farm. The banjo player's go-to for news, information and product source is the *Banjo Newsletter*, edited and published in Chilmark. As the editor, Don Nitchie, puts it, "The newsletter is devoted to all things banjo."

Mr. Nitchie is the second-generation editor of this forty-year-old publication. Hub Nitchie, Don's father and the inspirational high school history teacher, was part of a banjo-picking group that included his "uncle-in-law," Gale Huntington. The younger Nitchie entered into publishing the newsletter, circulating a chart-reading technique. Is there something in Chilmark water that invites musical creativity?

Nitchie points to the recent growth of the banjo's popularity. He notes that the core of the growth is among technologically savvy young people. In response to this shift and growth in the market, the newsletter is now available online.

The creative distance between Flip Scipio and Arlen Roth's Aquinnah and Bill Keith and Don Nitchie's Beetlebung Corner is small and shrinking.

Farther down the highway are younger, contemporary musicians. In 2004, Willy Mason, son of songwriter Jemima James, debuted with guitar and vocals, and brother Sam on drums, featuring his hits "Oxygen" and "So Long" on the album *Where the Humans Eat*. He opened for bands such as Radiohead and Beth Orton. Mason recorded the song "Pickup Truck" in a fundraising effort for the community radio station WVVY.

Willy Mason, son of Jemima James, exemplifies the Vineyard musician who managed to break loose. He grew up on the Vineyard and now has viable career prospects, both on-Island and off. *Courtesy of Dan Waters.*

Walking the streets of the Vineyard, "on any given summer weekend you might hear rock, folk, rap, reggae, and bluegrass," reported the *Boston Globe* on August 10, 2013. The article noted the "haunting songs of [Nina] Violet, 30, a fourth-generation islander," who began with the viola at the tender age of six and never looked back. She toured cross-country with Rob Myers's Kahoots band at the age of sixteen and Europe with Willy Mason at twenty. Her sound is a folksy soul, a unique blend of charm. She plays guitar, banjo, mandolin and keyboards.

Nina Violet is not the only musician to start on the Vineyard and find success offshore. The Keefe brothers came into their own in West Tisbury. Seb began playing drums at ten with his friend Willy Mason. Brother Joe Keefe chose guitar. Joe and Seb performed in their teen years and moved to Los Angeles after high school—and upward in their careers.

Their group, Family of the Year, traveled extensively, performed on Conan O'Brien's and Jimmy Kimmel's shows and played Nectar's on the Vineyard. The *Times* wrote, "The band's roots are truly on Martha's Vineyard."[93] The Keefe Brothers exemplify the Vineyard's successful musical exports.

West Tisbury youngsters who take up music are likely to be prodigies. Brad Tucker began playing guitar as an adolescent. He grew up in an atmosphere of guitar greats. As a kid, he used to sneak into the Ritz Café to catch the likes of Mike Benjamin and Johnny Hoy. "Tucker is perhaps an example of a phenomenon coined by Jim Parr, a longtime local music producer: 'You can't leave the Vineyard. You can try,' he said."[94] Tucker set off on a musical career with the sounds of folk, blues, bluegrass, ragtime and country; he headed for Nashville and joined the Woody Pines band, a "stripped down American roots" band, as lead guitar.

The Stringed Instrument Highway has other on-ramps, welcoming new, young musicians, providing opportunities and venues for them to express themselves along the way.

Chapter 18

HOUSEHOLD NAMES

High among the musical "seasonals" was world-famous coloratura soprano Beverly Sills (1929–2007), a longtime and devoted summer resident. Commuting to the rest of the world from the Vineyard allowed her to maintain her career and segue into her post-performance career, creating and administering mostly operatic programs.

At the same time, she threw herself into a range of activities typifying the Vineyard, such as the Saturday farmers' market in bucolic West Tisbury, where she bought fresh vegetables and sold those she grew.

The child of Jewish immigrants, Beverly Sills grew up in Brooklyn and was known to her fans as "Bubbles." Her husband, Peter Greenough, a Mayflower descendant with serious social credentials, built her a new home to replace his West Chop family homestead, cavernous and out of date in every respect.

Part of the allure of the Island for Ms. Sills was the array of friends from the arts she invited to her home. These included Barbara Walters, actor Joel Grey and Carol Burnett. She hosted dinner parties for Island family and friends. Among the latter were the William Styron family, the Mike Wallace family and the late Art Buchwald. Her friends included Island summer resident, composer, pianist (jazz and classical) and conductor Andre Previn.

In homage to Ms. Sills, we recount a comment she made when the La Scala Opera orchestra gave her a standing ovation at the end of her first rehearsal, the first time the honor was given. She remarked,

Indicative of her musical activities, Beverly Sills joined Andre Previn in a chamber music program at the Old Whaling Church in 1995. *Courtesy of Mark Lovewell.*

cheerily, "It's probably because Italians like big women, big breasts and big backsides." Nor can we avoid quoting the obituary in the *New York Times*: "She was more popular with the American public than any opera singer since Enrico Caruso, even among people who never set foot in an opera house."

A musician of a very different genre, Billy Joel, owned a house overlooking Menemsha Harbor, with his then-wife, supermodel Christie Brinkley and their daughter, Alexa. (The house played a small role in the movie *Sabrina.*) Joel, "the Piano Man" and member of the Rock and Roll Hall of Fame, must have found the Vineyard a comfortable site for his leisure, having grown up near a similar aquatic setting on Long Island.

Reflecting this culture, one of his hits, "The Downeaster Alexa," was written on the Vineyard as a protest against the mismanagement of the New England fisheries. It posits his views on the damaging effects of regulation of the fishing community in an area where he grew up and on his community of choice, Martha's Vineyard.

Billy Joel's Vineyard, however, was a place of rest and recreation. After nine years of marriage, he and Christie were divorced, and he sold their Vineyard house.

An important facet of the Vineyard culture is fundraising. Funding needs arise from a variety of Island nonprofit organizations: the Polly Hill Arboretum, Community Services, the Farm Institute, Featherstone Center for the Arts, the Martha's Vineyard Hospital and the YMCA, to mention but a few. Those needs are met with auctions, dinners and various functions for accessing Island residents' and visitors' checkbooks.

An artist of lofty renown who participated in a fundraising event on the Island is Ray Charles. A blind musical genius, his genres ranged over gospel, soul, country, pop and the blues. One of his signature songs, "Georgia on My Mind," brought him an invitation to the floor of the Georgia legislature, where he serenaded the legislators, a singular, symbolic honor for a Georgia-raised African American. "Georgia on My Mind" was adopted as the state song shortly thereafter. Tribute albums were done by Willie Nelson and Wynton Marsalis.

Doug Bell summered on the Vineyard in the 1960s, earning spending money as a duck pin boy at the Oak Bluffs bowling alley. He has enjoyed many memorable moments, "but NONE compare to opening for Ray Charles." He recalls, "The drive and energy could not be denied. It wouldn't have dawned on me as a suburban kid that I would have ever opened a show for Ray Charles!"

Doug Bell, who goes by the moniker "Professor," plays in Percy Sledge's band. "It all happened on Martha's Vineyard island. An acquaintance asked if we would like to do a charity show on the Vineyard and open for Ray Charles. That was it, a sold-out performance." It was for the Performing Arts Center.

FULL CIRCLE PRODUCTIONS
presents
AN EVENING WITH

RAY CHARLES

His Orchestra and the Famous Raelett's
Net proceeds to Benefit
AIDS Alliance of M. V. and M.V.R.H.S. P.A.C.
August 15, 1997
M.V.R.H.S. Performing Arts Center
Doors Open 6:00

Guest Appearance By
BELLEVUE CADILLAC

$100 General Admission

Ray Charles performed at the Martha's Vineyard Regional High School in 1997 to raise funds for the school and the AIDS Alliance of Martha's Vineyard. *Courtesy of Doug Bell.*

Percy Sledge's band warmed up the crowd and earned a generous critical review. After they left the stage, "My road manager and my wife crawled up above the catwalk and watched Ray Charles from above. He [Charles] was enamored of his Kurzweil computer keyboard and sat kicking his feet, and singing as only Ray could, his body lurching back and forth, smiling and becoming each and every song, body and soul!" Oh, that voice! Imagine looking down on Ray Charles during his performance; that takes chutzpah.

Professor Bell is no shrinking violet. After the show, he had himself introduced to Ray Charles and asked "if he thought it would be funny to be our chauffeur, and he said yes! Bill Johnson drove his vintage red caddie around to the front, and [we] waited like little kids, [but] soon our hopes were dashed by his handler/manager/walker, who said Mr. Charles has to go now, no time for photos." Professor Bell almost had a photo of Ray Charles in the driver's seat of a bright red Cadillac.

Bell does have a poster and photos of that historic event and "the thrill of meeting the man who wove deep soul and R&B into my tapestry. Songs like 'Night Time,' 'Unchain My Heart,' 'Georgia,' 'Hit the Road Jack,' 'Hallelujah I Just Love Her So,' 'I Can't Stop Loving You,' and 'You Don't Know Me'—the last song having a VERY different meaning at the time of civil rights. Ray Charles will always be the pinnacle 'pinch me' moment of my entire life. He never sang a false note, EVER."

Another memorable musical fundraiser was the collaboration among some remarkable musicians, philanthropists, performers and scientists to support efforts to further advance breakthroughs in kidney diagnosis and treatment.

Black Americans are disproportionally affected by kidney disease, and black philanthropy, as well as the non-black community, was called on to support the effort. The first-ever On the Vine Music Festival was held at several venues on the Island. The recipient of the proceeds of the festival was the Rambam Healthcare Campus in Haifa, Israel, where promising kidney research is being conducted by Dr. William Scorecki.

Headliners of the inaugural festival were kidney disease survivors Natalie Cole, Nat King Cole's daughter and a celebrated singer herself; Smokey Robinson, a master of soul and rhythm and blues; and comedian Richard Lewis. On the Vine ran for four days in August 2013 at premier venues on the Island, including the Tabernacle and Featherstone Center for the Arts.

Judy Collins recorded "Upon This Rock" with Lucy and Julie Simon; the song is on the *Best of the Vineyard Sound* album. *Courtesy of Alison Shaw.*

Arlo Guthrie (pictured in 1979) has often performed on the Vineyard, keeping alive the legend of his father, Woody. *Courtesy of Alison Shaw.*

No doubt the most glamorous and productive fundraiser, year after year, is the Martha's Vineyard Community Services Possible Dreams auction. Star names from the recent past like Walter Cronkite and Mike Wallace and current names such as Olga Hirshorn and Carly Simon raise hundreds of thousands of dollars at the August auction. All funds raised are donated to Martha's Vineyard Community Services.

Over the years, auction items have included sailing excursions with Walter Cronkite, tea with Patricia Neal, a singing hour with Carly Simon, yacht rides with Merv Griffen and tours of Washington's Hirshhorn Gallery. Are you convinced? The masterful master of ceremonies, year after year, was the late Art Buchwald.

Perhaps even more glamorous are the musical fundraisers. Big names in music come to the Island to draw and thrill the crowds of ticket-buying enthusiasts. The Agricultural Society's Livestock '95, featuring James Taylor and Carly Simon, met the society's needs in a trice. The pairing of Andre Previn with Beverly Sills at the Old Whaling Church in 1995 for the benefit of the Martha's Vineyard Preservation Trust was deemed a success.

One of the jewels in the crown of Island entertainment and fundraising has been the appearance of the Boston Pops. The Pops first appeared at the Vineyard in 1995 and annually until 2000, when the beneficiaries were the Tabernacle and the Martha's Vineyard Hospital. Beyond the excitement created by the Pops, the play list of the Pops was augmented, thrillingly, by Natalie Cole, Branford Marsalis, Gladys Knight and Vineyard icon Kate Taylor. Boston Pops nights are, invariably, quintessential Vineyard. Jerry Muskin and his wife attended, and he says, "I can confirm the review of one performance: 'The night was magical. The weather was beautiful. The location spectacular. The music delightful!'"

What better messenger for classical American music than Pulitzer Prize– and multiple Grammy Award–winning Wynton Marsalis and his Jazz at Lincoln Center orchestra. In recent back-to-back years, Wynton and his orchestra brought joy to sold-out Tabernacle audiences. These marvelous musicians also carried the jazz message to a young audience by providing a jazz familiarization course on the morning of the concert, conducted at the YMCA, the site of Alex's Place.

A *Vineyard Gazette* interview yielded this quote: "Mr. Marsalis said he loved playing at the Tabernacle last year. It's open, it has a deep community feeling. You can feel the warmth of the people. It's a lot of fun to play there. The evening glows." The producer of the event, Jack Stewart, in lauding the Vineyard crowd, noted that the audience was half white and half African American—a ratio found in only three or four venues around the world. "He wanted to come back," Mr. Stewart said. "He knows the crowd, he loved the vibe."

At the conclusion of this wondrous evening, Jerry Muskin penned a poem:

The Vineyard Performance

It had all the components of perfection:
A Vineyard evening non-pareil
A knowing audience
An ideal concert setting
&
The Lincoln Center Jazz Orchestra
with Wynton Marsalis at the helm
delivering generous helpings of
The Duke in music and prose
Thrill upon thrill
It couldn't help but overwhelm
And the evening delivered to the max
As they say these days "It met and
exceeded expectations"
I must admit these are opinions not facts
(but nonetheless true)
A source of pure joy part of any Marsalis program
is the skill and musicality of those who share
the stage with the master
Indeed the "side men" are masters themselves
Their status undiminished by their not having solos
on every piece nor does Marsalis himself.
If you love jazz you shoulda been there
The musical evening started where most end up

the orchestra started at the top of the
jazz repertoire playing that prophet of blues and style
Billy Strayhorn's "A-Train a' la the Duke"
The rest of the program matched the first offering
The program was to its end stellar and vibrant
At closing the audience rose and would not be silent
Whatta windup

Come back to the Vineyard soon, Wynton.

Chapter 19

THUS, GREATNESS

John Rogers (1927–2004) was an audio engineer. He had always been intrigued by electronics, and "when his daughter Nancy began taking piano lessons, he recorded her playing 'so she would hear her mistakes and her good points,'" reported Phyllis Meras in his *Vineyard Gazette* obituary.

Rogers's hobby became a vocation as he provided amplification for town meetings, weddings, services and concerts by the Martha's Vineyard Chamber Music Society and Island Community Chorus. "He recorded James Taylor in the 1960s performing at the Moon Cusser, Carly and Lucy Simon and movie actor and *Saturday Night Live* comedian Dan Ackroyd," Phyllis Meras wrote.

Besides amplifying and recording numerous events over the years, he fine-tuned his recordings, raising them to a high level. In his van, he stored any possible electronic equipment he might need, and he assisted seniors, befuddled by electronic equipment they did not comprehend.

Peter Simon has been closely association with the Vineyard music scene for much of his life. Besides organizing the No Nukes Concert at Allen Farm in 1978, he presented a radio program called *Good Vibrations* on WVOI in the

1970s and later ran a show entitled *Private Collection* for five years in the 1990s on WMVY.

Simon also produced two landmark albums entitled *Vineyard Sound* and *The Best of Vineyard Sound*, recordings of big-name musicians playing on the Vineyard, from Richie Havens to Entrain to Nina Violet to Kate Taylor. Those albums have become collectors' items, as they capture the spirit of music on Martha's Vineyard.

Peter Simon also edited *On the Vineyard*, a trilogy of books with essays by leading Vineyarders and his own photographs. Richard Skidmore compiled a summation of Vineyard musical history in that book.

For thirty years, WMVY was the Vineyard's commercial radio station. It converted to nonprofit status and was off the air for eighteen months, returning in May 2014, at 88.7 FM. The station is now listener supported, dependent on fundraising.

Laurel Redington works at WMVY. The transformation to a nonprofit status "served as a reality check, an identity adjustment." She says, "We serve the community." Of her playlist, she adds, "We can shape our own show." A typical pop radio station has about four hundred songs; a radio station with a variety of music has one thousand titles. MVY has eight thousand songs, online, available any time.

Laurel says, "We cater to the online audience, which is global, in seventeen countries and all fifty states." However, the local listening audience is also a big part of programming. (Her husband, Roy Whitaker, has a program on MVY called *Just Four Guys* about the Beatles.)

When Laurel Redington is not on air, she works at Alex's Place, at the YMCA. Concerts at Alex's Place can be simulcast on MVY and then archived. "Alex's Place is central to the Island, this substance-free environment," says Laurel. "Both sites involve a relationship based on mutual love of music."

Tony Lombardi, of Alex's Place, adds, "The tiniest footprint makes this statement all over the world. No one has done more for Martha's Vineyard than MVY. It's pretty heavy stuff."

Featherstone Center for the Arts provides a focus on the range of activities called "art." The center supports the arts year-round by providing courses, displays, presentations, opportunities for performances and off-Island specialists in many categories. One example of an off-Island artist brought to the Island to demonstrate and inspire the large and growing population of Island poets has been two-term poet laureate Billy Collins. (Jerry and his wife were privileged to sit under the tent to experience Collins's droll, penetrating and accessible poetry.)

Music is a prominent art form at Featherstone with Musical Mondays. Island musicians and audiences are grateful for the summer programs when picnic baskets and folding chairs abound. Island players of prominence and those seeking to join them play contemporary pop, rock and jazz on Monday and Thursday evenings. In addition, there is a Wednesday night ukulele event to accommodate the growing population of music lovers picking up that instrument. Musical Mondays at Featherstone has been ongoing nearly twenty years.

Featherstone has taken a step that puts the center into what some would call the "high culture" category with the Chamber Music Society. A well-known New York dance and opera impresario, Wendy Taucher, having spent several summers at the Vineyard, identified a demographic typified by well-educated, sophisticated, generous thinkers who would increasingly support opera at the Vineyard.

The year of this writing, a renowned cast will put on an abridged version of Mozart's *The Magic Flute* at Featherstone. As Jerry Muskin notes, "I'm happy to say, Carol and I experienced an exciting, brilliantly modified rendering of Rossini's *The Italian Girl in Algiers*." The opera programs are presented in a newly built opera stage with tiered seating.

Together, the Martha's Vineyard Chamber Music Society and the Featherstone Center for the Arts qualify the Vineyard as "the Classical Island." Not to be ignored is radio station WFCC, which plays classical music twenty-four/seven from the Cape.

Chapter 20

FROM TINY ACORNS

Rob Myers plays with Kahoots and Goodnight Louise. For twenty years, he has been part of the local music scene. Kahoots, formed in 1994, toured widely in its early years but now stays closer to home. Its sound is "part aggressive punk rock, part dance music, with some songs that are quiet and melancholy," says Myers.[95] He also plays in Good Night Louise, an American roots band.

He acknowledges disappointment in the number of local music venues that have closed down over the years, such as Che's Lounge, the Atlantic Connection, the Oyster Bar, the Pit Stop and Outerland. The *Gazette* noted, "The pulse of the scene is still in the bars and restaurants that regularly host live music," but they host small bands, and it's the food and drink that pay the bills.

"As a guy who's been down here a long time now, I'm realizing that this exact issue is probably the thing I care most about," Myers told the Gazette.[96] "It just doesn't make sense that there should be a lack of viable music venues." Myers has done his part, organizing the annual Best Fest festival, an end-of-season art and music gathering. And he has an optimistic take on the music scene, arguing that joining forces may bring people together to provide a venue. He suggests renovating the three old movie houses—the Capawok, the Strand and the Island—and revamping them as havens for music and art, as well as movies.

A key venue for musicians was lost when Aboveground Records closed after nearly twenty years of supplying Vineyarders with recorded music.

Mike Barnes's shop met the needs of the public unable to attend live shows or unwilling to buy online. Aboveground Records served the public and the musicians very well. It is sorely missed.

Looking at venues, Phil daRosa runs a production company that matches Island artists with Island sites. "We produce music events that benefit the Island community," says daRosa, who oversees TPS Presents, as well as his Oak Bluffs recording studio.

DaRosa thinks attracting big-name artists would support local musicians. The *Gazette* noted, "He recognizes the financial risk involved in bringing big name artists from off-Island to play here, but believes it's a crucial step toward elevating the scene to its true potential." DaRosa recalls, "Back in the '70s and '80s, Peter Tosh played here and Bonnie Raitt played here. All these amazing musicians were coming every season to the Vineyard. I'm trying to keep that alive."

Besides his production company and recording studio, Phil daRosa is a singer/songwriter; he plays bass with Dukes County Love Affair (DCLA), characterized by the *Globe* as "a gritty blues rock band with hip-hop elements." He is in a traditional reggae band, Island Thunder, and the electronic band Kodachrome.

Of fellow musicians, daRosa says he would like to emulate "folks like Johnny Hoy who have maintained the passion and drive to keep playing music live, and who love every moment of it." And he looks at the younger musicians, "like Willy Mason who have figured out a way to spread his music beyond this community into areas that really accept and love what he's doing." DaRosa is passionate about the creative process but simultaneously seeks to expand the listener base for local music.

What is missing on the Island, he says, is "support from the deeper pockets to bring world-class artists here." Local venues will not want to risk funds to finance an off-Island group without a guaranteed return.

He says, "I have hope that the Vineyard music scene will continue to grow into something that brings back artists from all over the world. My goal is to make every act that I book want to come back year after year and help this community build something special that will once again put Martha's Vineyard on the map as a magical place to come and share your music." He told the *Boston Globe*, "There are so many talented musicians here. It's a melting pot of musical talent. That's what motivates me and all of the stuff that I do. It really comes down to me just loving this music."

Sally and Ben Taylor performed at the Grange Hall in 2013. The legend continues. *Courtesy of Peter Simon.*

An element in the future of Vineyard music appears to be the genetic component. Time and again we see parents teaching their children; grandchildren following the sharps and flats of their forebears. Look at Mike Tinus and his wife, Rebecca: their daughters, Amalie and Mikayla, sang with the Minnesingers and show obvious musical talent. Milo Silva follows the musical measures of his father, Maynard. Willie Huntington's grandchildren excel in their field. Hudson Bausman follows his father. Willy Mason's mother is songstress Jemima James. Charlie Esposito plays with the Daytrippers; his son Tony follows his father's lead. Molly Conole sang with the Minnesingers and played a poignant tribute on her flute at the funeral for Pat Gregory; her daughter joined the Vineyard Haven Band on the oboe. The list of names is extensive and growing.

There is comfort in knowing the future of Vineyard music is in good hands, secure in the genetic makeup of its population. A key ingredient in the musical mix of Martha's Vineyard lies in the roots of the family tree, where parents share the joys of music with their progeny, encourage with their enthusiasm and extol the musical tradition on this magical musical island.

The musical family tree loops back on itself even as it moves upward and outward. We interviewed more than fifty musicians, but many more musical people are out there. Eric Johnson plays jazz with Jeremy Berlin and is a member of Daytrippers; Paul D. Adler, Jim Parr and Tom Major are influential players; Jeff Pratt and Barbara Dacey are contributors; and Jeremy Jones played with Maynard Silva. The list goes on. And new groups and singers continue to emerge. This story is a work in progress, ongoing, a snapshot in time.

Music keeps on keeping on. The Reflections of Peace Christmas Concert, produced by Kevin and Joanne Ryan, is an annual celebration, where local musicians perform. "Of all the musical events, we [musicians] like that the best," says Glenn Carpenter, who performs each year. Church music is alive and well. Three popular choirs are the West Tisbury Congregational Church, the Federated Church and Union Chapel in the summer.

Other groups spring up, perform sometimes below the radar screen and move on. Island Harmony, a barbershop quartet of Roger Lemenager, Kenny DeBettencourt, Dan Murphy and Jay Schofield, flourished and then faded. An a cappella group born of the Minnesingers recently spread its wings. Musical groups come and go, like the ebb and flow of the tide.

Balancing out all the newcomers is the Vineyard Haven Band, which has been tooting its own horn since 1868 and shows no signs of slowing down. Band members excel in the excitement of summer. At one Grand Illumination, banker and tenor Kevin Ryan sang the operatic piece "Nessun Norma," which wowed the crowd. Walter Cronkite led the band in the "Stars and Stripes Forever" at Owen Park, something he had always wanted to do. And at Ocean Park in mid-August, the band is at center stage as fireworks burst over the harbor.

An editorial in 1987 noted, "The spell of the band is strongest by far in the gazebo at Ocean Park in Oak Bluffs. Here, in the gathering dusk of summer Sunday evenings, the band draws families like moths to a shining lamp. Here, to the strains of 'Stars and Stripes Forever,' children and parents and grandparents march around the bandstand," looking like a Norman Rockwell *Saturday Evening Post* cover. The editorial concluded, "When we give thanks for the blessings of Island summer, we must always remember to include the Vineyard Haven Town Band."

The key to the future of music on Martha's Vineyard is the support and encouragement offered to those who have a musical interest and ability. Parents, teachers and mentors offer guidance for an ambition so intense it cannot be thwarted. Time and again, we heard musicians invoke their emotional attachment to the creative element of making music, performing, bringing forth the best of their sound, to share with an audience.

The story of Vineyard music includes the role of current musicians in welcoming the next generation. It includes providing available venues, from bars to clubs to performance centers, that encourage the artist to produce and invite the audience to appreciate the musical talents so ripe on the Vineyard.

Historically, Vineyard venues have excelled, from the Tivoli to the Tabernacle, from the Moon Cusser and Hot Tin Roof to Wintertide. Now Dreamland joins the Ritz and the Lampost in Oak Bluffs, Flatbread by the airport and the Atlantic in Edgartown to offer musical venues. Big-name musicians serve a receptive audience on the Vineyard but need a place to play. Alex's Place is viable, as is the PAC. MV Film Center has musical offerings.

The Singing Tiltons set the stage a century ago. The Taylor siblings have expanded the Vineyard's musical influence far beyond its shores. Local musicians find their voice before appreciative audiences. The beat goes on. This history of harmony lives on.

EPILOGUE

As we review the intertwining branches and limbs of the Vineyard musical tree, we discover musicians are nourished from many sources. Parents and teachers encourage their young to experiment singing or playing a guitar. Peers push their pals. And if the music is in the veins, then opportunity awaits and nothing can hold them back. Whether the singer/songwriter finds himself or herself in a tiny venue, an Island recording studio or facing fabulous contacts and contracts, opportunity awaits.

Joe Keenan recounts the tale of a boss who allows an employee, a budding musical prodigy, to leave work early for a gig. Jeremy Berlin shares the role of the elder statesman sharing experience. The press covers the novice, as well as the professional, in forays through Vineyard venues, from the Tivoli to the Hot Tin Roof, from the Ritz to the Chilmark Community Center. And the audience, receptive, eager, enthused, awaits that first strum of the guitar, the beat of a familiar song, the sheer exuberance of a musical experience.

We have tried to cover some of the fertile ground in which this musical tree flourishes. We know we have omitted musicians who have stature and promise, who contribute to the growth of the musical environment; for this we apologize. We recognize more young musicians are bursting forth, even as the seniors continue to pluck away.

The Vineyard is a vibrant source of various musical genes and genres, welcoming and rewarding. It has been an honor as well as an opportunity to explore these singular experiences.

NOTES

CHAPTER 1

1. Skidmore, "Tracing Island Music," 137.
2. Black Brook Singers of the Wampanoag Tribe of Aquinnah, January 17, 2008, Youtube.
3. Dan Adams for MVPBS, February 15, 2012.
4. *Vineyard Gazette*, August 27, 1846.
5. Ibid., August 1932.

CHAPTER 2

6. Huntington, *Songs the Whalemen Sang*, 16.
7. Ibid., 17.
8. Ibid., 18.
9. Mark Lovewell, *Vineyard Gazette*, January 5, 2006.
10. Melville, *Redburn*, 46.
11. Another book by Gale Huntington, *The Gam: More Songs the Whalemen Sang*, was published posthumously in 2014. *The Gam* is a sequel to Huntington's first book. It includes stories and poems of the whalemen.
12. Huntington, *Folksongs from Martha's Vineyard*, 18.

13.Sections of this piece appeared previously in the *Dukes County Intelligencer*, 2010.

14. Josiah Bardwell sponsored this event.

15. Tom Bardwell was the great-grandson of Francis Vincent Pease. Bardwell recorded his version of the band's history in 1997.

16. *A Centennial History*, 72.

17. Ibid., 60–61.

18. *Vineyard Gazette*, July 13, 1951.

19. Railton, *History of Martha's Vineyard*, 353.

20. Stuart MacMackin, "From the Tivoli to the Ocean View," *Intelligencer*, May 1983.

21. Railton, *History of Martha's Vineyard*, 353.

22. Skip Finley, *Vineyard Gazette*, May 9, 2013. Finley went on to say, "His [Will Hardy's] grandson Sterling Smith gave the [Martha's Vineyard] museum the Tivoli Girl Album of sheet music of 14 waltzes including such favorites as 'Vineyard Isle,' 'That Wonderful Island of Mine' (1928), 'Here Comes the Sankaty with My Best Girl on Board (1917).'"

Chapter 3

23. Huntington, *Folksongs from Martha's Vineyard*, 12.

24. Ibid., 13.

25. Burroughs, *Zeb: Celebrated Schooner Captain*, 29.

26. Huntington, *Folksongs from Martha's Vineyard*, 13.

27. Ibid., 31.

28. Ibid., 17.

29. Ibid.

30. Welcome Tilton had two children, Alton and Tom. Tom had two children, Les and Mildred. Gale Huntington met Mildred and fell in love with her and with folksongs. They were married in 1932.

31. Huntington, *Folksongs from Martha's Vineyard*, 53.

32. *Vineyard Gazette*, July 9, 1943.

33. Ibid., August 27, 1943.

34. Ibid., February 25, 1944.

35. Ibid., May 18, 1944.

36. Ibid., August 27, 1943.

Chapter 4

37. Richter, *Fiddles, Harmonicas and Banjos*, 40. The book is an examination of the reasons, methods and conclusions of Benton's foray into music, which was like an iceberg. Until Richter's book, we could see only the one-eighth above the water.
38. Ibid., 44.
39. Ibid., 47.
40. Ibid., 39.
41. Lee, *More Vineyard Voices*, 146.
42. Jerry Muskin defines a tone poem as a single-movement musical composition for orchestra, inspired by an extra-musical concept.
43. Shirley Mayhew, "Dig That Island Sound," *Martha's Vineyard Magazine*, Winter–Spring 2013–14.
44. Kate Taylor responded to a request for recollections of her musical heritage.

Chapter 5

45. Dave Seward was interviewed for this project.
46. Kate Taylor responded to a request for recollections of her musical heritage.
47. A moon cusser would lure boats onto a rocky shore by hanging a lantern that resembled the moon. Once the boat was grounded, the thief stole the cargo. The logo of the Moon Cusser was a lantern; the club was decorated in a barn board and burlap theme. The phone number was MV #211.
48. Tony Omer, "The Moon Cusser Coffee Shop Remembered by the Folk Music Loving Sewards," *Martha's Vineyard Times*, August 29, 2013.
49. The Charles River Valley Boys were from Cambridge, Massachusetts, while the Clancy Brothers were an Irish folk music group.
50. Jonah Lipsky, "When Going Viral Meant Passing Posters, Folkies All Flocked to the Moon Cusser," *Vineyard Gazette*, July 29, 2012.
51. David Gude's partner was Jessie Benton Lyman, daughter of Thomas Hart Benton. Their son was Anthony Gude.
52. Tom Rush responded to a request for recollections about his Vineyard musical experiences.
53. Kate Taylor responded to a request for recollections of her musical heritage.
54. *Vineyard Gazette*, February 25, 1966.

CHAPTER 6

55. *New York Times*, January 31, 2006.

56. Mary Grauerholz, "At Home with Hugh and Jeanne Taylor: Thriving on the Rhythm of Martha's Vineyard," *Boston Globe*, August 21, 2003.

57. Judy Wyle was interviewed for this project.

CHAPTER 8

58. Bob Hammond was interviewed for this project.

59. Ibid.

60. Linda Black, "The Beat Goes On," *Martha's Vineyard Magazine*, August 2009.

61. Ivy Ashe, "They Came, They Saw, They Moved In: Exploring the Vineyard's Counterculture Roots," *Vineyard Gazette*, August 1, 2013.

62. Linda Black, "The Beat Goes On," *Martha's Vineyard Magazine*, August 2009.

63. Chris Burrell, "Under One (Hot Tin) Roof," *Martha's Vineyard Magazine*, July 2006.

64. Kate Taylor responded to a request for recollections of her musical heritage.

65. *Vineyard Gazette*, June 1, 1982.

66. Ibid., May 21, 1982.

67. Chris Burrell, "Under One (Hot Tin) Roof," *Martha's Vineyard Magazine*, July 2006.

68. Chris Burrell, *Vineyard Gazette*, March 22, 2001.

69. Chris Burrell, "Under One (Hot Tin) Roof," *Martha's Vineyard Magazine*, July 2006.

70. Katie Carroll, Chilmark Town Column, *Martha's Vineyard Times*, December 5, 2012.

CHAPTER 9

71. Sherman Goldstein was interviewed for this project.

72. Susanna Sturgis, squattersspeakeasy.com, May 11, 2013.

73. Buchwald's column, dated August 14, 1995, was entitled "War and Peace and Music."

Chapter 10

74. Ellis Paul is a nationally known modern troubadour from Maine, who harkens back to the days of Pete Seeger and Woody Guthrie, singing folksongs to the young.
75. Alex's Place is a center of teen activity at the Y. It was built in memory of Alexandra Gagnon.
76. Naomi Pallas, "Wintertide Is Back with Singer/Songwriter Ellis Paul," *Martha's Vineyard Times*, August 29, 2012.

Chapter 11

77. *Vineyard Gazette*, July 17, 2008.
78. Ortiz was a coast guardsman stationed on the Vineyard during World War II and met his wife, Mary, at a USO; she worked at the Van Ryper model shipyard during the war and died in 2014.
79. Julia Wells, obituary for Maynard Silva, *Vineyard Gazette*, July 17, 2008.

Chapter 12

80. Heeremans, *The Stick*, 98.
81. *Vineyard Gazette*, July 19, 2012.
82. Tom Dunlop, "The A Capella Boys of Summer," *Martha's Vineyard Magazine*, July 2008.

Chapter 13

83. The Duke Ellington Society, based in New York City, is organized to celebrate the Duke, his music and that of his collaborator, Billy Strayhorn.
84. George White was the treasurer of Fisk College in the 1870s. He organized the Jubilee Singers in a fundraising effort, which proved very successful.
85. From an interview with Andrew Ward, who wrote a book entitled *Dark Midnight When I Rise: The Story of the Fisk Jubilee Singers*.

Chapter 14

86. Elaine Pace, "Dee Stevens," *Martha's Vineyard Magazine*, July 2010.
87. Ibid.
88. *Vineyard Gazette*, May 16, 2013.
89. *Martha's Vineyard Times*, October 8, 2013.
90. *Vineyard Gazette*, July 22, 1941.

Chapter 17

91. Michael Seccombe, "It's Just Wood Until Guitar Fixer for the Stars (and the Soldiers) Flip Scipio Makes It Sing," *Martha's Vineyard Magazine*, July 2008.
92. Ibid.
93. Maddy Berg, "Nectars a Stop on Local Brothers' Successful Journey," *Martha's Vineyard Times*, July 6, 2011.
94. *Boston Globe*, August 10, 2013.

Chapter 20

95. Derek Schwartz, "Vineyard's Got Talent, but Musicians Say Off-Island Mix Essential," *Vineyard Gazette*, June 6, 2014.
96. Ibid.

BIBLIOGRAPHY

Books

Burroughs, Polly. *Zeb: Celebrated Schooner Captain of Martha's Vineyard*. Guilford, CT: Globe Pequot Press, 2005; originally published in 1972.

Heeremans, Harold. *The Stick: Music the Hard Way*. N.p.: self-published, 1978.

Huntington, Gale. *Folksongs from Martha's Vineyard*. Vol. 8. Edited by Edward Ives. Orono: Northeast Folklore Society, University of Maine, 1966.

———. *The Gam: More Songs the Whalemen Sang*. Northfield, MN: Loomis House Press, Camsco Music, 2014.

———. *Songs the Whalemen Sang*. Mystic, CT: Mystic Seaport Museum, 2006; originally published in 1964.

Lee, Linsey. *More Vineyard Voices*. Edgartown, MA: Martha's Vineyard Museum, 2005.

Melville, Herman. *Redburn*. New York: Harper & Brothers, 1849.

Muskin, Jerry. *Meanderings*. N.p.: Xlibris, 2012.

Oak Bluffs Historical Commission. *A Centennial History of Cottage City*. Oak Bluffs, MA: Martha's Vineyard Printing, 2007.

Railton, Arthur. *The History of Martha's Vineyard*. Edgartown, MA: Dukes County Historical Society, 2006.

Richter, Annett Claudia. *Fiddles, Harmonicas and Banjos: Thomas Hart Benton and His Role in Constructing Popular Notions of American Folk Music and Musicians*. St. Paul: University of Minnesota Press, 2008.

Skidmore, Richard. "Tracking Island Music: A Selective History." In *On the Vineyard III*, by Peter Simon. Chilmark, MA: Simon Press, 2000.

Periodicals

Boston Globe.
Dukes County Intelligencer.
Martha's Vineyard Magazine.
Martha's Vineyard Times.
Rolling Stone.
Vineyard Gazette.

Albums

Alaimo, John. *It's the Good Life.* Engineered, mixed and mastered by Jim Parr; recorded at ParrAudio, Martha's Vineyard.

Huntington, Gale. *Folksongs from Martha's Vineyard.* 1957.

James, Jemima. *Nothing New.* Produced by Jemima James and Bob Brown; mastered by Phil daRosa. 2014.

Keady, Kevin. *The Best of Kevin Keady.* Recorded and mixed by Jim Parr, produced by Mike Benjamin.

King, Carole, and James Taylor. *Live at the Troubadour.* 2010.

Lovewell, Mark. *Martha's Vineyard Folksongs.* Recorded and mastered at Audiolutions, Vineyard Haven, MA. 2005.

———. *Sea Songs of Martha's Vineyard.* Recorded and mixed at Parr Audio, Martha's Vineyard. 2002.

Simon, Peter. *The Best of the Vineyard Sound.* 2009.

INDEX

ABOUT THE AUTHORS

From age eleven until he went off to college, Thomas Dresser edited a monthly newspaper. He taught elementary school for ten years, then switched from eight year-olds to eighty-year-olds and worked as a nursing home administrator for twenty years.

Since relocating to Martha's Vineyard in 1995, Tom has driven a school bus and a tour bus, served on local boards and is a member of the Martha's Vineyard Museum (historical society). *Music on Martha's Vineyard* is his seventh book with The History Press.

He may be contacted at thomasdresser.com.

Jerry Muskin, the poet, is an octogenarian with a long list of careers and positions. A university professor emeritus (not in literature), he has also been a bureaucrat, an entrepreneur, an army officer, an executive, a band member (trumpet), an inventor, a truck driver, a member of the board of the Chamber Music Society and a consultant to government and industry. Each year, he plays his bugle to open the Martha's Vineyard Agricultural Society Fair. More significant than any of the foregoing is that he is a devoted husband and a proud and loving father and grandfather.